What **MAXnotes**® *Will Do for You*

This book is intended to help you absorb the essential contents and features of William Shakespeare's *A Midsummer Night's Dream* and to help you gain a thorough understanding of the work. Our book has been designed to do this more quickly and effectively than any other study guide.

For best results, this **MAXnotes** book should be used as a companion to the actual work, not instead of it. The interaction between the two will greatly benefit you.

To help you in your studies, this book presents the most up-to-date interpretations of every scene of the actual work, followed by questions and fully explained answers that will enable you to analyze the material critically. The questions also will help you to test your understanding of the work and will prepare you for discussions and exams.

Meaningful illustrations are included to further enhance your understanding and enjoyment of the literary work. The illustrations are designed to place you into the mood and spirit of the work's settings.

The **MAXnotes** also include summaries, character lists, explanations of plot, and scene-by-scene analyses. A biography of the author, an introduction to the language, and discussion of the work's historical context will help you put this literary piece into the proper context of what is taking place.

The use of this study guide will save you the hours of preparation time that would ordinarily be required to arrive at a complete grasp of this work of literature. You will be well prepared for classroom discussions, homework, and exams. The guidelines that are included for writing papers and reports on various topics will prepare you for any added work which may be assigned.

The **MAXnotes** will take your grades "to the max."

Larry B. Kling
Chief Editor

Contents

> **Each Scene includes List of Characters, Summary, Analysis, Study Questions and Answers, and Suggested Essay Topics.**

MAXnotes® are simply the best - but don't just take our word for it...

"... I have told every bookstore in the area to carry your MAXnotes. They are the only notes I recommend to my students. There is no comparison between MAXnotes and all other notes ..."

    – High School Teacher & Reading Specialist,
    Arlington High School, Arlington, MA

"... The two MAXnotes titles that I have used have been very, very useful in helping me understand the subject matter reviewed. Thank you for creating the MAXnotes series ..."

    – Student, Morrisville, PA

A Glance at Some of the Characters

Hermia

Lysander

Helena

Demetrius

Nick Bottom

Oberon

Titania

Robin Goodfellow

Introduction

The Life and Work of William Shakespeare

The details of William Shakespeare's life are sketchy, mostly mere surmise based upon court or other clerical records. His parents, John and Mary (Arden), were married about 1557; she was of the landed gentry, and he was a yeoman—a glover and commodities merchant. By 1568, John had risen through the ranks of town government and held the position of high bailiff, which was a position similar to a mayor. William, the eldest son and the third of eight children, was born in 1564, probably on April 23, several days before his baptism on April 26 in Stratford-upon-Avon. Shakespeare is also believed to have died on the same date—April 23—in 1616.

It is believed that William attended the local grammar school in Stratford where his parents lived, and that he studied primarily Latin, rhetoric, logic, and literature. Shakespeare probably left school at age 15, which was the norm, to take a job, especially since this was the period of his father's financial difficulty. At age 18 (1582), William married Anne Hathaway, a local farmer's daughter who was eight years his senior. Their first daughter (Susanna) was born six months later (1583), and twins, Judith and Hamnet, were born in 1585.

Shakespeare's life can be divided into three periods: the first 20 years in Stratford, which include his schooling, early marriage, and fatherhood; the next 25 years as an actor and playwright in London; and the last five in retirement in Stratford where he enjoyed the moderate wealth gained from his theatrical successes. The years linking the first two periods are marked by a lack of information about Shakespeare, and are often referred to as the "dark years."

At some point during the "dark years," Shakespeare began his career with a London theatrical company, perhaps in 1589, for he was already an actor and playwright of some note by 1592. Shakespeare apparently wrote and acted for numerous theatrical companies, including Pembroke's Men, and Strange's Men, which later became the Chamberlain's Men, with whom he remained for the rest of his career.

In 1592, the Plague closed the theaters for about two years, and Shakespeare turned to writing book-length narrative poetry. Most notable were "Venus and Adonis" and "The Rape of Lucrece", both of which were dedicated to the Earl of Southampton, whom scholars accept as Shakespeare's friend and benefactor despite a lack of documentation. During this same period, Shakespeare was writing his sonnets, which are more likely signs of the time's fashion rather than actual love poems detailing any particular relationship. He returned to playwriting when theaters reopened in 1594, and did not continue to write poetry. His sonnets were published without his consent in 1609, shortly before his retirement.

Amid all of his success, Shakespeare suffered the loss of his only son, Hamnet, who died in 1596 at the age of 11. But Shakespeare's career continued unabated, and in London in 1599, he became one of the partners in the new Globe Theater, which was built by the Chamberlain's Men.

Shakespeare wrote very little after 1612, which was the year he completed *Henry VIII*. It was during a performance of this play in 1613 that the Globe caught fire and burned to the ground. Sometime between 1610 and 1613, Shakespeare returned to Stratford, where he owned a large house and property, to spend his remaining years with his family.

William Shakespeare died on April 23, 1616, and was buried two days later in the chancel of Holy Trinity Church, where he had been baptized exactly 52 years earlier. His literary legacy included 37 plays, 154 sonnets, and five major poems.

Incredibly, most of Shakespeare's plays had never been published in anything except pamphlet form, and were simply extant as acting scripts stored at the Globe. Theater scripts were not regarded as literary works of art, but only the basis for the performance. Plays were simply a popular form of entertainment for all layers of society in Shakespeare's time. Only the efforts of two of Shakespeare's company, John Heminges and Henry Condell, preserved his 36 plays (minus *Pericles*, the thirty-seventh).

The Theater of William Shakespeare

Shakespeare's theater was very different from today's in both form and management. Actors were considered vagabonds until The Act of 1572, which declared acting a legitimate profession PROVIDING the player (actor) was under the patronage of a peer of the realm. In 1576, the first public playhouse, The Theater, was built in London. It was during this time that the acrobatic, farcical work done by the wandering troupes of actors in the yards of inns began to transform itself into actors performing in plays. Now there were "companies," groups of eight to ten men who invested their capital in a common stock of plays (and the apparel necessary to stage them) and shared the profits in proportion to the capital each invested. Periodically, plays (which were considered part of the company's stock) were sold to raise capital; *A Midsummer Night's Dream* was offered to publishers, along with *The Merchant of Venice, Much Ado about Nothing,* and *Henry IV* in 1600 by Lord Chamberlin's Men in an attempt to raise capital to build the Globe. The company also had two or three boy apprentices trained for the female parts since women did not act. There might also be novices or old timers with no capital to invest who were hired for minor parts (as Shakespeare was initially).

The resident dramatist wrote plays meant to display the strong points of the lead actors, keeping the acting skills of the other players in mind since that was what was going to show a profit for the company. The actors had almost absolute control over what was written for them by the dramatist commissioned by the company (which then owned the play), the resident dramatist, or through their own updating of plays they already owned. A different play was presented each afternoon of the week, with a new one introduced every two weeks or so. Summer was traditionally for touring, spring and autumn were for the local London theater, and winter was for rehearsals, with the exception of Christmas when a play was presented to the Queen.

The theater itself, specifically the Globe, was an open-air structure with an internal courtyard surrounded by seating arranged in balconies. The stage, a bare platform surrounded on three sides by the audience, had one setting which could be manipulated slightly by use of artificial rocks or countryside. There was a second stage, lower than the first, which was used for more formal, indoor scenes. These were cold, drafty, massive areas holding a cross-section of society and containing between two and three thousand people, half of them standing. The majority of the audience was made up of poor city workers. These people stood closest to the stage, which gave them ample opportunity to throw things at the actors when displeased, hiss, boo, pointedly clap, noticeably shout, and pass remarks to the actors as they were performing. What we now call the dressing room (then called the tiring house) was behind a curtain across the back of the stage. The front of the stage was an open area without the curtain we are used to seeing raised to signal the beginning of the play. The partial roof over the stage was often painted with the moon and stars to signify heaven, while the floor had trapdoors in it to allow hellish creatures to appear. Soliloquies, asides, long speeches, and descriptive poetry were all used to establish the setting of the play in the absence of painted scenery and artificial lighting. Later theaters, such as Blackfriars, were more intimate, holding only two to three hundred people with the wealthy paying the higher price for seats closest to the stage (the opposite pricing situation of the Globe). The theater was enclosed with seats for all, making tickets more costly, which meant a wealthier, more educated audience usually attended.

Shakespeare's Language

Shakespeare's language can create a strong pang of intimidation, even fear, in a large number of modern-day readers. Fortunately, however, this need not be the case. All that is needed to master the art of reading Shakespeare is to practice the techniques of unraveling uncommonly-structured sentences and to become familiar with the poetic use of uncommon words. We must realize that during the 400-year span between Shakespeare's time and our own, both the way we live and speak has changed. Although most of his vocabulary is in use today, some of it is obsolete, and what may be most confusing is that some of his words are used today, but with slightly different or totally different meanings. On the stage, actors readily dissolve these language stumbling blocks. They study Shakespeare's dialogue and express it dramatically in word and in action so that its meaning is graphically enacted. If the reader studies Shakespeare's lines as an actor does, looking up and reflecting upon the meaning of unfamiliar words until the real voice is discovered, he or she will suddenly experience the excitement, the depth and the sheer poetry of what these characters say.

Shakespeare's Sentences

In English, or any other language, the meaning of a sentence greatly depends upon where each word is placed in that sentence. "The child hurt the mother" and "The mother hurt the child" have opposite meanings, even though the words are the same, simply because the words are arranged differently. Because word position is so integral to English, the reader will find unfamiliar word arrangements confusing, even difficult to understand. Since Shakespeare's plays are poetic dramas, he often shifts from average word arrangements to the strikingly unusual so that the line will conform to the desired poetic rhythm. Often, too, Shakespeare employs unusual word order to afford a character his own specific style of speaking.

Today, English sentence structure follows a sequence of subject first, verb second, and an optional object third. Shakespeare, however, often places the verb before the subject, which reads, "Speaks he" rather than "He speaks." Solanio speaks with this inverted structure in *The Merchant of Venice* stating, "I should be still/ Plucking the grass to know where sits the wind" (Bevington edition, I, i, ll.17-19), while today's standard English word order would have the clause at the end of this line read, "where the wind sits." "Wind" is the subject of this clause, and "sits" is the verb. Bassanio's words in Act Two also exemplify this inversion: "And in such eyes as ours appear not faults" (II, ii, l. 184). In our normal word order, we would say, "Faults do not appear in eyes such as ours," with "faults" as the subject in both Shakespeare's word order and ours.

Inversions like these are not troublesome, but when Shakespeare positions the predicate adjective or the object before the subject and verb, we are sometimes surprised. For example, rather than "I saw him," Shakespeare may use a structure such as "Him I saw." Similarly, "Cold the morning is" would be used for our "The morning is cold." Lady Macbeth demonstrates this inversion as she speaks of her husband: "Glamis thou art, and Cawdor, and shalt be/What thou art promised" (*Macbeth*, I, v, ll. 14-15). In current English word order, this quote would begin, "Thou art Glamis, and Cawdor."

In addition to inversions, Shakespeare purposefully keeps words apart that we generally keep together. To illustrate, consider Bassanio's humble admission in *The Merchant of Venice*: "I owe you much, and, like a wilful youth,/That which I owe is lost" (I, i, ll. 146-147). The phrase, "like a wilful youth," separates the regular sequence of "I owe you much" and "That which I owe is lost." To understand more clearly this type of passage, the reader could rearrange these word groups into our conventional order: I owe you much and I wasted what you gave me because I was young and impulsive. While these rearranged clauses will sound like normal English, and will be simpler to understand, they will no longer have the desired poetic rhythm, and the emphasis will now be on the wrong words.

As we read Shakespeare, we will find words that are separated by long, interruptive statements. Often subjects are separated from verbs, and verbs are separated from objects. These long interruptions can be used to give a character dimension or to add an element of suspense. For example, in *Romeo and Juliet*, Benvolio describes both Romeo's moodiness and his own sensitive and thoughtful nature:

> I, measuring his affections by my own,
> Which then most sought, where most might not be found,
> Being one too many by my weary self,
> Pursu'd my humour, not pursuing his,
> And gladly shunn'd who gladly fled from me. (I, i, ll. 126-130)

In this passage, the subject "I" is distanced from its verb "Pursu'd." The long interruption serves to provide information which is integral to the plot. Another example, taken from *Hamlet,* is the ghost, Hamlet's father, who describes Hamlet's uncle, Claudius, as

> ...that incestuous, that adulterate beast,
> With witchcraft of his wit, with traitorous gifts—
> O wicked wit and gifts, that have the power
> So to seduce—won to his shameful lust
> The will of my most seeming virtuous queen. (I, v, ll. 43-47)

From this we learn that Prince Hamlet's mother is the victim of an evil seduction and deception. The delay between the subject, "beast," and the verb, "won," creates a moment of tension filled with the image of a cunning predator waiting for the right moment to spring into attack. This interruptive passage allows the play to unfold crucial information and thus to build the tension necessary to produce a riveting drama.

While at times these long delays are merely for decorative purposes, they are often used to narrate a particular situation or to enhance character development. As *Antony and Cleopatra* opens, an interruptive passage occurs in the first few lines. Although the delay is not lengthy, Philo's words vividly portray Antony's military prowess while they also reveal the immediate concern of the drama. Antony is distracted from his career, and is now focused on Cleopatra:

>   ...those goodly eyes,
> That o'er the files and musters of the war
> Have glow'd like plated Mars, now bend, now turn
> The office and devotion of their view
> Upon a tawny front.... (I, i, ll. 2-6)

Whereas Shakespeare sometimes heaps detail upon detail, his sentences are often elliptical, that is, they omit words we expect in written English sentences. In fact, we often do this in our spoken conversations. For instance, we say, "You see that?" when we really mean, "Did you see that?" Reading poetry or listening to lyrics in music conditions us to supply the omitted words and it makes us more comfortable reading this type of dialogue. Consider one passage in *The Merchant of Venice* where Antonio's friends ask him why he seems so sad and Solanio tells Antonio, "Why, then you are in love" (I, i, l. 46). When Antonio denies this, Solanio responds, "Not in love neither?" (I, i, l. 47). The word "you" is omitted but understood despite the confusing double negative.

In addition to leaving out words, Shakespeare often uses intentionally vague language, a strategy which taxes the reader's attentiveness. In *Antony and Cleopatra*, Cleopatra, upset that Antony is leaving for Rome after learning that his wife died in battle, convinces him to stay in Egypt:

> Sir, you and I must part, but that's not it:
> Sir you and I have lov'd, but there's not it;
> That you know well, something it is I would—
> O, my oblivion is a very Antony,
> And I am all forgotten. (I, iii, ll. 87-91, emphasis added)

In line 89, "...something it is I would" suggests that there is something that she would want to say, do, or have done. The intentional vagueness leaves us, and certainly Antony, to wonder. Though this sort of writing may appear lackadaisical for all that it leaves out, here the vagueness functions to portray Cleopatra as rhetorically sophisticated. Similarly, when asked what thing a crocodile is (meaning Antony himself who is being compared to a crocodile), Antony slyly evades the question by giving a vague reply:

> It is shap'd, sir, like itself, and it is as broad as it hath
> breadth. It is just so high as it is, and moves with it own
> organs. It lives by that which nourisheth it, and, the
> elements once out of it, it transmigrates. (II, vii, ll. 43-46)

This kind of evasiveness, or doubletalk, occurs often in Shakespeare's writing and requires extra patience on the part of the reader.

Shakespeare's Words

As we read Shakespeare's plays, we will encounter uncommon words. Many of these words are not in use today. As *Romeo and Juliet* opens, we notice words like "shrift" (confession) and "holidame" (a holy relic). Words like these should be explained in notes to the text. Shakespeare also employs words which we still use, though with different meaning. For example, in *The Merchant of Venice*, "caskets" refer to small, decorative chests for holding jewels. However, modern readers may think of a large cask instead of the smaller, diminutive casket.

Another trouble modern readers will have with Shakespeare's English is with words that are still in use today, but which mean something different in Elizabethan use. In *The Merchant of Venice*, Shakespeare uses the word "straight" (as in "straight away") where we would say "immediately." Here, the modern reader is unlikely to carry away the wrong message, however, since the modern meaning will simply make no sense. In this case, textual notes will clarify a phrase's meaning. To cite another example, in *Romeo and Juliet*, after Mercutio dies, Romeo states that the "black fate on moe days doth depend" (emphasis added). In this case, "depend" really means "impend."

Shakespeare's Wordplay

All of Shakespeare's works exhibit his mastery of playing with language and with such variety that many people have authored entire books on this subject alone. Shakespeare's most frequently used types of wordplay are common: metaphors, similes, synecdoche and metonymy, personification, allusion, and puns. It is when Shakespeare violates the normal use of these devices, or rhetorical figures, that the language becomes confusing.

A metaphor is a comparison in which an object or idea is replaced by another object or idea with common attributes. For example, in *Macbeth*, a murderer tells Macbeth that Banquo has been murdered, as directed, but that his son, Fleance, escaped, having witnessed his father's murder. Fleance, now a threat to Macbeth, is described as a serpent:

There the grown serpent lies, the worm that's fled
Hath nature that in time will venom breed,
No teeth for the present. (III, iv, ll. 29-31, emphasis added)

Similes, on the other hand, compare objects or ideas while using the words "like" or "as." In *Romeo and Juliet,* Romeo tells Juliet that "Love goes toward love as schoolboys from their books" (II, ii, l. 156). Such similes often give way to more involved comparisons, "extended similes." For example, Juliet tells Romeo:

'Tis almost morning, I would have thee gone,
And yet no farther than a wonton's bird,
That lets it hop a little from his hand
Like a poor prisoner in his twisted gyves,
And with silken thread plucks it back again,
So loving-jealous of his liberty.
(II, ii, ll. 176-181, emphasis added)

An epic simile, a device borrowed from heroic poetry, is an extended simile that builds into an even more elaborate comparison. In *Macbeth,* Macbeth describes King Duncan's virtues with an angelic, celestial simile and then drives immediately into another simile that redirects us into a vision of warfare and destruction:

                    ...Besides this Duncan
Hath borne his faculties so meek, hath been
So clear in his great office, that his virtues
Will plead like angels, trumpet-tongued, against
The deep damnation of his taking-off;
And pity, like a naked new-born babe,
Striding the blast, or heaven's cherubim, horsed
Upon the sightless couriers of the air,
Shall blow the horrid deed in every eye,
That tears shall drown the wind....
(I, vii, ll. 16-25, emphasis added)

Shakespeare's employs other devices, like synecdoche and metonymy, to achieve "verbal economy," or using one or two words to express more than one thought. Synecdoche is a figure of speech using a part for the whole. An example of synecdoche is using the word boards to imply a stage. Boards are only a small part of the materials that make up a stage, however, the term boards has become a colloquial synonym for stage. Metonymy is a figure of speech using the name of one thing for that of another which it is associated. An example of metonymy is using crown to mean the king (as used in the sentence "These lands belong to the crown"). Since a crown is associated with or an attribute of the king, the word crown has become a metonymy for the king. It is important to understand that every metonymy is a synecdoche, but not every synecdoche is a metonymy. This rule is true because a metonymy must not only be a part of the root word, making a synecdoche, but also be a unique attribute of or associated with the root word.

Synecdoche and metonymy in Shakespeare's works is often very confusing to a new student because he creates uses for words that they usually do not perform. This technique is often complicated and yet very subtle, which makes it difficult of a new student to dissect and understand. An example of these devices in one of Shakespeare's plays can be found in *The Merchant of Venice* (I, v, ll. 30-32). In warning his daughter, Jessica, to ignore the Christian revelries in the streets below, Shylock says:

> Lock up my doors; and when you hear the drum
> And the vile squealing of the wry-necked fife,
> Clamber not you up to the casements then. . .

The phrase of importance in this quote is "the wry-necked fife." When a reader examines this phrase it does not seem to make sense; a fife is a cylinder-shaped instrument, there is no part of it that can be called a neck. The phrase then must be taken to refer to the fife-player, who has to twist his or her neck to play the fife. Fife, therefore, is a synecdoche for fife-player, much as boards is for stage. The trouble with understanding this phrase is that "vile squealing" logically refers to the sound of the fife, not the fife-player, and the reader might be led to take fife as the instrument because of the parallel reference to "drum" in the previous line.

The best solution to this quandary is that Shakespeare uses the word fife to refer to both the instrument and the player. Both the player and the instrument are needed to complete the wordplay in this phrase, which, though difficult to understand to new readers, cannot be seen as a flaw since Shakespeare manages to convey two meanings with one word. This remarkable example of synecdoche illuminates Shakespeare's mastery of "verbal economy."

Shakespeare also uses vivid and imagistic wordplay through personification, in which human capacities and behaviors are attributed to inanimate objects. Bassanio, in *The Merchant of Venice*, almost speechless when Portia promises to marry him and share all her worldly wealth, states "my blood speaks to you in my veins..." (III, ii, l. 176). How deeply he must feel since even his blood can speak. Similarly, Portia, learning of the penalty that Antonio must pay for defaulting on his debt, tells Salerio, "There are some shrewd contents in yond same paper/That steals the color from Bassanio's cheek" (III, ii, ll. 243-244).

Another important facet of Shakespeare's rhetorical repertoire is his use of allusion. An allusion is a reference to another author or to an historical figure or event. Very often Shakespeare alludes to the heroes and heroines of Ovid's *Metamorphoses*. For example, in Cymbeline an entire room is decorated with images illustrating the stories from this classical work, and the heroine, Imogen, has been reading from this text. Similarly, in *Titus Andronicus*, characters not only read directly from the *Metamorphoses*, but a subplot re-enacts one of the *Metamorphoses's* most famous stories, the rape and mutilation of Philomel.

Another way Shakespeare uses allusion is to drop names of mythological, historical and literary figures. In *The Taming of the Shrew*, for instance, Petruchio compares Katharina, the woman whom he is courting, to Diana (II, i, l. 55), the virgin goddess, in order to suggest that Katharina is a man-hater. At times, Shakespeare will allude to well-known figures without so much as mentioning their names. In *Twelfth Night*, for example, though the Duke and Valentine are ostensibly interested in Olivia, a rich countess, Shakespeare asks his audience to compare the Duke's emotional turmoil to the plight of Acteon, whom the goddess Diana transforms into a deer to be hunted and killed by Acteon's own dogs:

Duke:	That instant was I turn'd into a hart,
	And my desires, like fell and cruel hounds,
	E'er since pursue me.
	[...]
Valentine:	But like a cloistress she will veiled walk,
	And water once a day her chamber round....

(I, i, l. 20 ff.)

Shakespeare's use of puns spotlights his exceptional wit. His comedies in particular are loaded with puns, usually of a sexual nature. Puns work through the ambiguity that results when multiple senses of a word are evoked; homophones often cause this sort of ambiguity. In *Antony and Cleopatra*, Enobarbus believes "there is mettle in death" (I, ii, l. 146), meaning that there is "courage" in death; at the same time, mettle suggests the homophone metal, referring to swords made of metal causing death. In early editions of Shakespeare's work there was no distinction made between the two words. Antony puns on the word "earing," (I, ii, ll. 112-114) meaning both plowing (as in rooting out weeds) and hearing: he angrily sends away a messenger, not wishing to hear the message from his wife, Fulvia: "...O then we bring forth weeds,/ when our quick minds lie still, and our ills told us/Is as our earing." If ill-natured news is planted in one's "hearing," it will render an "earing" (harvest) of ill-natured thoughts. A particularly clever pun, also in *Antony and Cleopatra*, stands out after Antony's troops have fought Octavius's men in Egypt: "We have beat him to his camp. Run one before,/And let the queen know of our gests" (IV, viii, ll. 1-2). Here "gests" means deeds (in this case, deeds of battle); it is also a pun on "guests," as though Octavius' slain soldiers were to be guests when buried in Egypt.

One should note that Elizabethan pronunciation was in several cases different from our own. Thus, modern readers, especially Americans, will miss out on the many puns based on homophones. The textual notes will point up many of these "lost" puns, however.

Shakespeare's sexual innuendoes can be either clever or tedious depending upon the speaker and situation. The modern reader should recall that sexuality in Shakespeare's time was far more complex than in ours and that characters may refer to such things as masturbation and homosexual activity. Textual notes in some editions will point out these puns but rarely explain them. An example of a sexual pun or innuendo can be found in *The Merchant of Venice* when Portia and Nerissa are discussing Portia's past suitors using innuendo to tell of their sexual prowess:

> Portia: I pray thee, overname them, and as thou
>   namest them, I will describe them, and
>   according to my description level at my
>   affection.
> Nerrisa: First, there is the Neapolitan prince.
> Portia: Ay, that's a colt indeed, for he doth nothing but
>   talk of his horse, and he makes it a great
>   appropriation to his own good parts that he can
>   shoe him himself. I am much afeard my lady his
>   mother played false with the smith.
>
> (I, ii, ll. 35-45)

The "Neapolitan prince" is given a grade of an inexperienced youth when Portia describes him as a "colt." The prince is thought to be inexperienced because he did nothing but "talk of his horse" (a pun for his penis) and his other great attributes. Portia goes on to say that the prince boasted that he could "shoe him [his horse] himself," a possible pun meaning that the prince was very proud that he could masturbate. Finally, Portia makes an attack upon the prince's mother, saying that "my lady his mother played false with the smith," a pun to say his mother must have committed adultery with a blacksmith to give birth to such a vulgar man having an obsession with "shoeing his horse."

It is worth mentioning that Shakespeare gives the reader hints when his characters might be using puns and innuendoes. In *The Merchant of Venice*, Portia's lines are given in prose when she is joking, or engaged in bawdy conversations. Later on the reader will notice that Portia's lines are rhymed in poetry, such as when she is talking in court or to Bassanio. This is Shakespeare's way of letting the reader know when Portia is jesting and when she is serious.

Shakespeare's Dramatic Verse

Finally, the reader will notice that some lines are actually rhymed verse while others are in verse without rhyme; and much of Shakespeare's drama is in prose. Shakespeare usually has his lovers speak in the language of love poetry which uses rhymed couplets. The archetypal example of this comes, of course, from Romeo and Juliet:

> The grey-ey'd morn smiles on the frowning night,
> Check'ring the eastern clouds with streaks of light,
> And fleckled darkness like a drunkard reels
> From forth day's path and Titan's fiery wheels.
>
> (II, iii, ll. 1-4)

Here it is ironic that Friar Lawrence should speak these lines since he is not the one in love. He, therefore, appears buffoonish and out of touch with reality. Shakespeare often has his characters speak in rhymed verse to let the reader know that the character is acting in jest, and vice-versa.

Perhaps the majority of Shakespeare's lines are in blank verse, a form of poetry which does not use rhyme (hence the name blank) but still employs a rhythm native to the English language, iambic pentameter, where every second syllable in a line of ten syllables receives stress. Consider the following verses, and note the accents and the lack of end-rhyme:

> The síngle ánd pecúliar lífe is bóund
> With áll the stréngth and ármor óf the mínd
>
> (Hamlet, III, iii, ll. 12-13)

The final syllable of these verses receives stress and is said to have a hard, or "strong," ending. A soft ending, also said to be "weak," receives no stress. In *The Tempest*, Shakespeare uses a soft ending to shape a verse that demonstrates through both sound (meter) and sense the capacity of the feminine to propagate:

and thén I lóv'd thee
And shów'd thee áll the quálitíes o' th' ísle,
The frésh spríngs, bríne-pits, bárren pláce and fértile.

(I, ii, ll. 338-40)

The first and third of these lines here have soft endings.

In general, Shakespeare saves blank verse for his characters of noble birth. Therefore, it is significant when his lofty characters speak in prose. Prose holds a special place in Shakespeare's dialogues; he uses it to represent the speech habits of the common people. Not only do lowly servants and common citizens speak in prose, but important, lower class figures also use this fun, at times ribald, variety of speech. Though Shakespeare crafts some very ornate lines in verse, his prose can be equally daunting, for some of his characters may speechify and break into doubletalk in their attempts to show sophistication. A clever instance of this comes when the Third Citizen in *Coriolanus* refers to the people's paradoxical lack of power when they must elect Coriolanus as their new leader once Coriolanus has orated how he has courageously fought for them in battle:

We have power in ourselves to do it, but it is a power that we have no power to do; for if he show us his wounds and tell us his deeds, we are to put our tongues into those wounds and speak for them; so, if he tell us his noble deeds, we must also tell him our noble acceptance of them. Ingratitude is monstrous, and for the multitude to be ingrateful were to make a monster of the multitude, of the which we, being members, should bring ourselves to be monstrous members.

(II, ii, ll. 3-13)

Notice that this passage contains as many metaphors, hideous though they be, as any other passage in Shakespeare's dramatic verse.

When reading Shakespeare, paying attention to characters who suddenly break into rhymed verse, or who slip into prose after speaking in blank verse, will heighten your awareness of a character's mood and personal development. For instance, in

Antony and Cleopatra, the famous military leader Marcus Antony usually speaks in blank verse, but also speaks in fits of prose (II, iii, ll. 43-46) once his masculinity and authority have been questioned. Similarly, in *Timon of Athens*, after the wealthy lord Timon abandons the city of Athens to live in a cave, he harangues anyone whom he encounters in prose (IV, iii, l. 331 ff.). In contrast, the reader should wonder why the bestial Caliban in *The Tempest* speaks in blank verse rather than in prose.

Implied Stage Action

When we read a Shakespearean play, we are reading a performance text. Actors interact through dialogue, but at the same time these actors cry, gesticulate, throw tantrums, pick up daggers, and compulsively wash murderous "blood" from their hands. Some of the action that takes place on stage is explicitly stated in stage directions. However, some of the stage activity is couched within the dialogue itself. Attentiveness to these cues is important as one conceives how to visualize the action. When Iago in *Othello* feigns concern for Cassio whom he himself has stabbed, he calls to the surrounding men, "Come, come:/Lend me a light" (V, i, ll. 86-87). It is almost sure that one of the actors involved will bring him a torch or lantern. In the same play, Emilia, Desdemona's maidservant, asks if she should fetch her lady's nightgown and Desdemona replies, "No, unpin me here" (IV, iii, l. 37). In *Macbeth*, after killing Duncan, Macbeth brings the murder weapon back with him. When he tells his wife that he cannot return to the scene and place the daggers to suggest that the king's guards murdered Duncan, she castigates him: "Infirm of purpose/Give me the daggers. The sleeping and the dead are but as pictures" (II, ii, ll. 50-52). As she exits, it is easy to visualize Lady Macbeth grabbing the daggers from her husband.

For 400 years, readers have found it greatly satisfying to work with all aspects of Shakespeare's language—the implied stage action, word choice, sentence structure, and wordplay—until all aspects come to life. Just as seeing a fine performance of a Shakespearean play is exciting, staging the play in one's own mind's eye, and revisiting lines to enrich the sense of the action, will enhance one's appreciation of Shakespeare's extraordinary literary and dramatic achievements.

Historical Background

In order for the title to have any meaning for the contemporary student of Shakespeare's play, its origin must be explained. At the time the play was written, only three seasons were observed: autumn, winter, and summer—which included what we now consider spring and began in March. Therefore, the play, whose action takes place on the eve of May Day, actually is in midsummer as Shakespeare knew it. This was the time of year when animals were traditionally let out to pasture and the spirits of nature were thought to be abroad. The action takes place in the fairy wood, which may be what the "dream" part of the title refers, although it may refer to another common custom, the divining by midsummer dreams and flowers who one's lover is or whether one's lover is faithful, just as the characters in the play do. It was also customary on May Day (May 1st) to greet the day with a sunrise service that includes songs to emphasize hope and cheerfulness.

As was usual for a dramatist of his time, most of Shakespeare's plays were not original. This is not to say he plagiarized, rather that plays were based on other, earlier works by masters such as the ones Shakespeare studied in grammar school: Ovid, Plautus, Terence, and Chaucer. For Shakespeare, the poetry and the event were much more important than the characters in his plays. There are several theories about this but the preponderant one is that Puck is the imagination's way of ordering the random. It could be said that Puck (from English rustic folklore) is the gateway between the imaginative elements and reality as we know it. Curiously enough, Bottom is the only human who can see the imaginative (fairy) elements.

The play-within-the-play seems to be Shakespeare's version of a dramatist and actor's worst nightmare. Lines are forgotten, cues missed, conversation carried on between the actors and the audience, and the actors' efforts laughed at. In addition, the audience loudly and freely carries on conversations during the production. It is also a parody of his own *Romeo and Juliet* which was written just prior to this play. Remembering that Shakespeare was both an actor and a dramatist may give us some insight into the behavior of actual audiences at the Globe.

This particular play, commonly thought to have been commissioned for the wedding of Elizabeth Carey and Thomas, the Son of Henry, Lord Berkeley, is Shakespeare's most fully articulated. We have the lovers who are either in love or out of it with no middle ground: Theseus and Hippolyta, Hermia and Lysander, and Helena and Demetrius, the fairy world, Puck as the gateway between the fantasy and real world, Bottom as the human "invited" into the fairy world, and the play within a play. This internal play, ending unhappily for its pair of lovers, serves to show the three happily united or reunited couples in the larger play just how lucky they are. Music was used extensively in the fairy scenes since they are in pentameter couplet and other free forms which are suitable for singing. In keeping with his progressive treatment of female characters (although played by young boys), Shakespeare makes a great deal of the distinction between Helena and Hermia by constantly referring to their opposite physical attributes and temperaments while making very little distinction between their male lovers, Lysander and Demetrius. He is also careful to make apparent the distinction between the court and the craftspeople, except, of course, when Bottom is beloved by Titania.

This play was first printed in The Quarto Edition in 1600, although the printing of plays was not encouraged since the thinking at that time was that no one would bother to actually attend the theater to see a play once they could read it instead. Licenses were granted to both the Globe and The Blackfriars permitting them to "reform" Shakespeare's plays. Apparently they did because when Samuel Pepys saw the play for the first time, in its reformed version, in 1662, he was appalled by the play but loved the dancing (in the fairy scenes). In 1692, Thomas Betterton produced an operatic adaptation with music by Henry Purcell.

Other musical adaptations in the eighteenth century were Richard Leveridge's *Comic Masque of Pyramus and Thisbe* in 1716, J. F. Lampe's revision of Leveridge's production in 1745 as Pyramus and Thisbe, and Charles Johnson's using the play within the play and *As You Like It* to produce *Love in a Forest* in 1723. In 1755, new songs were introduced in the production of *The Fairies* which was abbreviated by George Colman in 1763 to become *A Fairy Tale.*

In 1816, the acclaimed Convent Garden was the site for Frederick Reynold's musical version. By the Victorian era, Mendelssohn's music became the focal point and the original text was cut heavily for Reynold's production. This practice of musical productions as opposed the play Shakespeare wrote continued well into the twentieth century.

Master List of Characters

Hermia—*a young woman in love with Lysander but ordered by her father to marry Demetrius*

Helena—*Hermia's friend from childhood who is in love with Demetrius*

Lysander—*the youth in love with Hermia*

Demetrius—*the man chosen by Egeus for his daughter, Hermia, to marry despite her love for Lysander*

Egeus—*Hermia's father who insists upon his paternal right to choose her husband*

Theseus—*the duke of Athens; engaged to Hippolyta*

Hippolyta—*engaged to Theseus*

Philostrate—*master of the revel (celebration for Theseus and Hippolyta's wedding)*

Nick Bottom (the weaver)—*manager of the play-within-a-play and portrays Pyramus in it; becomes the object of Titania's love*

Peter (the carpenter)—*author and director of the play-within-the-play*

Francis Flute (the bellows mender)—*unwillingly plays the role of Thisbe in the play-within-the-play*

Tom Snout (the tinker)—*portrays a wall in the play-within-the-play*

Robin Starveling (the tailor)—*portrays the moon in the play-within-the-play*

Snug (the joiner)—*portrays the lion in the play-within-the-play because he roars well*

Oberon—*king of the fairies; married to Titania*

Titania—*queen of the fairies; married to Oberon*

Robin Goodfellow (Puck)—*a hobgoblin in Oberon's service*

Peaseblossom, Cobweb, Mote, and Mustardseed—*Titania's fairies*

Summary of the Play

Theseus and Hippolyta are to wed at the new moon and Philostrate has been ordered to have a revel prepared for the wedding. Several local craftsmen agree to write and produce a play for the revel. Egeus brings his daughter, Hermia, to Theseus for judgment since he is convinced that her choice of husband, Lysander, has bewitched her into choosing him. According to Athenian law, a father may decide who his daughter marries; if she does not obey, she may be put to death or ordered to a nunnery for the rest of her life. As she is well aware, her father has chosen Demetrius. The craftsmen repair to the woods to rehearse at the same time Lysander and Hermia meet there to plan their elopement. Hermia and Lysander confide in Helena, who has previously been jilted by Demetrius and wants to win him back. Helena, in turn, tells Demetrius of the young lovers' meeting.

Fairies have come from India to bless Theseus' wedding and are haunting the same wood where the craftsmen and lovers plan to meet. Oberon is quarreling with Titania over her continued possession of a changeling; in retaliation for his wife's actions, Oberon sends Puck to gather the flower necessary to make a love juice. This love juice will cause the one who has it squeezed into his/her eye while asleep to fall in love with the first being seen upon waking. Helena follows Demetrius into the wood as he attempts to find the lovers, thereby disturbing Oberon who then orders Puck to squeeze the love juice into the eye of the youth who disturbed him. Oberon describes Demetrius by his clothes, but Puck finds Lysander asleep near Hermia and thinks this is the youth Oberon meant. Puck anoints Demetrius' eye while Oberon does the same to Titania. When Helena, still following the unwilling Demetrius, finds Lysander she wakes him and becomes the object of his love. While Lysander is pursuing Helena, Hermia awakens and searches for him.

The craftsmen arrive in the haunted wood to rehearse. Puck is still nearby and plays a trick on Nick Bottom by putting an ass's head on him. The others flee in terror, but Bottom remains singing to keep up his courage. His song awakens the anointed Titania, who immediately falls in love with him. Hermia happens upon Demetrius and accuses him of murdering Lysander and then runs away. Demetrius is exhausted and falls asleep whereupon Puck anoints his eyes. Lysander and Helena arrive quarreling which wakes Demetrius who then falls in love with Helena. The two men begin competing for her love. Hermia hears the noise and joins them, only to accuse Helena of stealing Lysander's love. The men go off to find a place to fight and Helena, afraid of Hermia, runs away with Hermia in pursuit. Oberon orders Puck to make the four lovers sleep and reanoint Lysander as he sleeps, so that he will fall in love with Hermia once again.

Titania continues her amorous pursuit of Bottom as the mismatched lovers fall asleep. Oberon gains possession of the changeling and removes the enchantment from his wife. He orders Puck to take the ass's head off Bottom. As the sun rises, Hippolyta and Theseus enter the wood to hunt, see the sleeping lovers, and awaken them with hunting horns. Egeus brings his suite again, but Demetrius is now in love with Helena and leaves Hermia to Lysander. Theseus is so pleased at this that he invites each pair of rightly matched lovers to be wed during his own wedding. Bottom wakes up thinking the whole experience has been a dream.

The craftsmen give their play, which they think is wonderful. At midnight, the lovers go to sleep and Oberon and Titania, with their fairies, take over the palace. They dance, sing, bless the sleepers, and leave. Puck remains to apologize and request applause from the audience.

Estimated Reading Time

Using The New Folger Library edition, reading will take approximately three hours (including the introductory and concluding material). Keeping in mind that readers will take more or less time, depending on what they choose to dwell upon and their reading rate. The time allotted for each section is as follows: introductory material – 45 minutes; Act I – 20 minutes; Act II – 30 minutes;

Act III – 55 minutes; Act IV – 10 minutes; Act V – 10 minutes; concluding material – 10 minutes. Because of the puns, double entendres, poetic description, and unfamiliar syntax, it is suggested you read the play itself at least twice. Readers should read the play once to familiarize themselves with Shakespeare's use of the English language and then again read to better grasp the plot with its twists and turns and to firmly establish the role of each character in the plot.

Act I

Act I, Scene 1

New Characters:

Theseus: *duke of Athens; engaged to Hippolyta*

Hippolyta: *engaged to Theseus*

Egeus: *Hermia's father who insists upon his paternal right to choose her husband*

Lysander: *the youth in love with Hermia*

Demetrius: *the man chosen by Egeus for his daughter, Hermia, to marry despite her love for Lysander*

Hermia: *a young woman in love with Lysander but ordered by her father to marry Demetrius*

Helena: *Hermia's friend from childhood who is in love with Demetrius*

Philostrate: *the master of the revel (celebration for Theseus and Hippolyta's wedding)*

Summary

As Theseus awaits his wedding day, Egeus brings Hermia, Lysander, and Demetrius to Theseus, who agrees she must marry Demetrius or be sentenced to death or a nunnery since it is the

father's right to decide who his daughter will marry. Lysander has an aunt who lives out of Theseus' jurisdiction, so the lovers agree to meet in the wood in order to plan their escape to the aunt's house. They tell Helena of their plans, but she is still in love with Demetrius and thinks if she tells him of her love he will no longer love Hermia.

Analysis

Plautus and Terence both strongly influenced Shakespeare's writing. These Roman writers used typical characters for their new comedies; a young man (Lysander), a father who opposes the wishes of his child (Egeus), and a tricky slave (in this case, a non-human — Puck). Shakespeare adhered to Plautus' and Terence's three-part structure of play writing, which is composed of: part one – a situation which is the opposite of the "right" one is set up; part two – since it is not the usual situation, complications follow; and part three – the opening situation is "righted," usually through some gimmick in the plot. The plot is very much akin to contemporary soap operas in that the boy loves a girl, her father vetoes the match, and then the boy somehow wins the girl with the father's approval. In line 136, Shakespeare clearly states his use of Plautus' and Terence's methods and succinctly foreshadows the moral of the entire play, "The true course of love never did run smooth."

In this initial section of the three-part structure, the situation is set with the "wrong" person being chosen. Hermia is a head-strong young woman ready not only to risk her father's wrath by choosing Lysander over Demetrius, but she also risks her life, since death is one of the possible punishments available to her father. Hermia is also willing to risk her sexual and sensual life since her father's alternative punishment is banishment to a nunnery, which would mean no sex, pregnancy, childbirth, motherhood, or sensual pleasures. Demetrius also chooses the "wrong" person. He had once wooed Helena, but now courts Hermia, Helena's close friend since childhood. Even Theseus seems to choose the "wrong" person since he won Hippolyta by waging war on her, however, they do truly seem to be happy that they are going to be wed and are impatient for the four days until the new moon. In addition, unlike the other couples, there are no other suitors to complicate their relationship.

Study Questions

1. Why has Theseus ordered a revel?
2. What does he promise Hippolyta?
3. Why does Egeus bring Hermia, Lysander, and Demetrius to Theseus?
4. Why does Theseus tell Hermia to come to terms with her father's choice of husband for her?
5. What is Hermia's decision?
6. Why does Theseus lead Egeus and Demetrius away?
7. What is Lysander's plan?
8. Why does Helena want to be like Hermia?
9. Why do Hermia and Lysander tell Helena the plan?
10. What does Helena intend to do with this information?

Answers

1. Theseus, Duke of Athens, has ordered a revel to celebrate his marriage to Hippolyta, Queen of the Amazons, who he won through battle. The marriage is to take place in four days when there is a new moon. He desires to "... Stir up the Athenian youth to merriments. Awake the pert and nimble spirit of mirth."

2. Theseus promises Hippolyta that their marriage will be one of joy, unlike the warring he used to win her, by declaring, "...But I will wed thee in another key...."

3. Egeus brings Hermia, Lysander, and Demetrius to Theseus because he (Egeus) wants Hermia to marry Demetrius. Against Egeus' will, Hermia wants to marry Lysander. Egeus wants Theseus to invoke the law requiring that a daughter marry the husband her father chooses for her or face the consequences: death or banishment to a nunnery. This is illus-

trated when Egeus says, "...I beg the ancient privilege of Athens...."

4. Theseus tells Hermia to come to terms with the husband her father has chosen for her or "...prepare to die for disobedience to your father's will, ... or on Diana's alter to protest for aye austerity and single life."

5. Hermia chooses to enter a nunnery rather than marry someone other than Lysander, who she feels is her true love. She protests, "So will I grow, so live, so die, my lord, ere I will yield my virgin patent up...."

6. Theseus leads Egeus and Demetrius away saying, "...But, Demetrius, come, and come Egeus, you shall go with me," in order to speak with them privately. This is also a device to allow the actors to leave the stage so that Lysander and Hermia may plot alone.

7. Lysander's plan is that Hermia and he will flee to his aunt's house, in a place where, "...the sharp Athenian law cannot pursue..." them and where they may be married.

8. Helena wants Hermia to, "...teach me how you look and with what art ..." because Demetrius loves Hermia and Helena wants his love for her own. She thinks that if only she were like Hermia, she could have his love.

9. Hermia and Lysander tell Helena their plan because Helena complains to Hermia that Demetrius wants only Hermia. They reassure Helena that Hermia will no longer be available to Demetrius and, as Hermia promises, "... he shall no more see my face," since Hermia and Lysander are going to elope.

10. Helena intends to tell Demetrius that Hermia is going to elope with Lysander in the hope that he will pursue them, only to realize it is Helena he really loves at which point Helena will "... have his sight thither and back again."

Suggested Essay Topics

1. How does the exposition in Act I, Scene i seem to support

Lysander's statement that, "The course of true love never did run smooth?"

2. Helena tells Hermia, "My ear should catch your voice; my eye your eye…." Considering Hermia's present relationship and Helena's past relationship with Demetrius, explain how this exemplifies Shakespeare's use of the first part of Plautus' and Terence's three-part method of writing comedic plays.

3. How does Egeus' statement (referring to Hermia), "And she is mine, and all my right of her I do estate unto Demetrius," demonstrate that Shakespeare is using this character to fulfill the role of the opposing father, which is a typical character in the New Comedy of Plautus and Terence?

Act I, Scene 2

New Characters:

Peter Quince (the carpenter): *author and director of the play-within-the-play*

Nick Bottom (the weaver): *manager of the play-within-the-play and is Pyramus in it; becomes the object of Titania's love*

Francis Flute (the bellows mender): *unwillingly plays the role of Thisbe in the play-within-the-play*

Snug (the joiner): *portrays the lion in the play-within-the-play because he roars well*

Robin Starveling (the tailor): *portrays the moon in the play-within-the-play*

Tom Snout (the tinker): *portrays a wall in the play-within-the play*

Summary

The craftsmen meet with Quince, the director, to assign the roles for the play—"The most lamentable comedy and most cruel death of Pyramus and Thisbe"—they are going to present at the

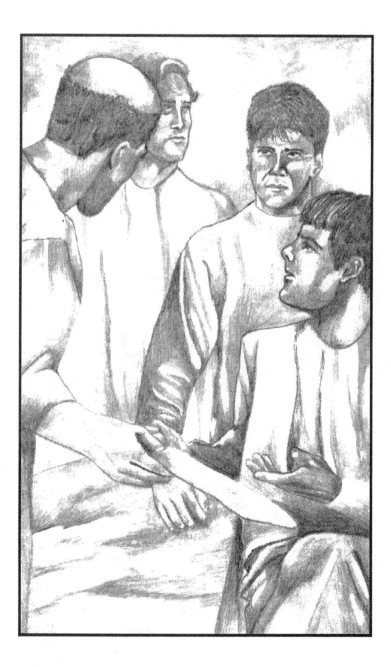

revel in honor of Theseus' and Hippolyta's wedding during the new moon in four days. Bottom is to play the lover, Pyramus, although he would prefer to be Thisbe or the Lion and professes that he will make the audience cry. Flute is to play the lady, Thisbe, but is worried because he is growing a beard, however, this will be covered by a mask so it is not the problem he thinks it is. Starveling is to play Thisbe's mother and the Moon. Snout is to be Pyramus' father and the Wall. Quince will play Thisbe's father. Snug, who is to be the Lion, is worried he will need more time to memorize his lines but he needs only roar. After some discussion of what beard Bottom should wear as his costume, the men agree to meet in the wood to rehearse since they would be too easily distracted or interrupted should they rehearse in the city.

Analysis

In this scene, we begin to differentiate the craftsmen from one another. Bottom, who predicts his extraordinary job of acting and states his preference for the "fun" parts, seems to be the clown of the group. Snug, worrying that he will not learn his part in time, seems well aware of his limitations. Flute, on the other hand, is the literalist wondering how he can play a woman if he is growing a beard. Quince is all business and reassuring as well, making certain each is comfortable with his role and ironing out any problems they may foresee with their parts. Starveling and Snout are perfectly acquiescent, asking no questions and making no comments.

Study Questions

1. Why do the craftsmen meet?
2. Why is Quince the one assigning the roles?
3. What is Bottom's reaction to his assigned role?
4. What is Flute's misgiving about his assignment?
5. Why does Bottom want to play Flute's role?
6. What is Snug's worry?
7. Why does Bottom want to play Snug's role?

8. What do Quince and Bottom caution about the role of the Lion?

9. Why does Quince insist Bottom play Pyramus?

10. Where are the men to meet next?

Answers

1. The craftsmen meet to assign and discuss the roles they will have, "... to play in our interlude before the Duke and the Duchess on his wedding day at night." Quince wrote and is directing this play for Theseus' and Hippolyta's wedding, which is to be held during the new moon, four days hence.

2. Quince is the person assigning the roles because he wrote the play with, "...every man's name which is thought fit ..." for certain roles. As the director, it is his job to cast the actors in the parts for which they are most suited—an easy job for him since he is also the dramatist (playwright).

3. Bottom's reaction to his assigned role is that he wants to know who Pyramus is and, when told, proclaims he will have everyone crying with his portrayal of this lover who dies. To quote, "I will move storms; I will condole in some measure."

4. Flute's misgiving about his assignment is that he is growing a beard and women don't have beards—so how can he play the part of a woman? As he protests, "Nay, faith, let not me play a woman. I have a beard coming."

5. Bottom requests, "...let me play Thisbe, too," because he wants to wear the mask the character will be wearing and use a small voice, as Flute will have to do to portray a woman.

6. Snug's worry is that he will not have enough time to memorize his lines since he is, "slow of study" as he phrases it, and the play is to be in only four days.

7. Bottom requests, "Let me play the lion too," so that he may roar as Snug will have to for this part. Bottom seeks the exciting or "fun" parts for himself, possibly giving us a hint as to his nature.

8. Quince and Bottom caution the Lion not to frighten the ladies in the audience because, "…that were enough to hang us all."

9. Quince insists Bottom, "…must needs play Pyramus," because he has both the bearing and the face of this character. Remembering that Quince wrote the play with Bottom in mind for the role of Pyramus will also help explain Quince's insistence on Bottom playing this particular role.

10. The men are next to meet, "At the Duke's Oak…" which happens to be in the haunted wood, although the craftsmen are not aware that the fairies are now in residence there.

Suggested Essay Topics

1. Quince admonishes Bottom that if he were to have the part of the lion and roar too loudly, he "…would frighten the Duchess and the ladies that they would shriek…." What does this tell us about the Elizabethan view of women? Validate your opinion with clues from the text.

2. In talking about the beard to go with his costume, Bottom says, "…either your straw-color beard, your orange-tawny beard, your purple-in-grain beard, or your French-crown-color beard, your perfit yellow." In your opinion, and taking hints from his conversations with Quince, just how much experience has Bottom had with acting?

3. The name of the play is "The most lamentable comedy and most cruel death of Pyramus and Thisbe." Considering that Bottom has already presented himself as something of a clown, why do you think it appropriate he play the lead in a play with this title?

Act II

Act II, Scene 1

New Characters:

Robin Goodfellow (Puck): *a hobgoblin in Oberon's service*

Oberon: *king of the fairies; married to Titania*

Titania: *queen of the fairies; married to Oberon*

Summary

Puck and one of the fairies come upon each other in the wood. The fairy ascertains that Puck is that spirit who is mischievous and plays all sorts of tricks on humans and animals alike. Oberon and Titania enter with their various attendants from opposite sides of the wood (stage), still deep in their quarrel about Titania's refusing to relinquish the changeling—a child secretly exchanged for another in infancy—she had brought from India with her since his mother had been her friend and died in childbirth. Each accuses the other of infidelities and each takes a turn at denying these accusations. Titania remarks that Nature is at odds with itself due to their argument and leaves her husband before the argument becomes even worse. Oberon vows to punish his wife and does so by sending Puck to find a certain flower called "love-in-idleness" with which to make a love juice. With this juice he intends to anoint the sleeping Titania's eye so that when she awakens she will fall in love

with the first creature she sees. His intention is not to remove the spell until she gives him the changeling.

As Oberon awaits Puck's return, Demetrius enters the wood with Helena in pursuit. Oberon, being invisible, is privy to Demetrius' imploring Helena to leave him alone and Helena's begging Demetrius to be with her in any capacity. When Puck returns with the flower, Oberon instructs him to anoint Demetrius—describing him by his Athenian clothing—with the love juice so that Demetrius will love Helena as she loves him. Puck promises to do as he is bid.

Analysis

Shakespeare uses the stage to make the point that Oberon and Titania are at opposite sides of this argument by having them enter from opposite sides of the stage. The accusations they make of each other, that Oberon has had an affair with Hippolyta and that Titania has had one with Theseus, are preposterous since they are both in Athens to bless and celebrate the wedding of these two people. Shakespeare pokes fun at the convention that the play begin with lovers choosing the "wrong" people, in addition to being an extremely good foil to show that Nature—meaning all of the natural world including the people in it—is at odds with itself since the king and queen of the fairies are arguing. This keeps with the Elizabethan idea that the elemental (fairy) kingdom is the creator and, hence, controller of nature—particularly the woods where fairies were thought to abide.

Helena's pursuit of Demetrius also begins Shakespeare's use of devices to sort out the lovers so that they eventually achieve the love of the "right" people. Since this play is a love comedy, this use of an obstacle to delay the union of one of the heroes and one of the heroines is to be expected. What makes this part of the play something of a tragic comedy is that Demetrius had wooed, and won, Helena before Egeus chose him for a son-in-law and he fell in love with Hermia who (as we already know) is planning to elope with her own choice of husband, Lysander.

In keeping with plot designs for New Comedy of the Romans, Plautus and Terence, we already have a complication to the first part. Not only has the situation been set with the young people

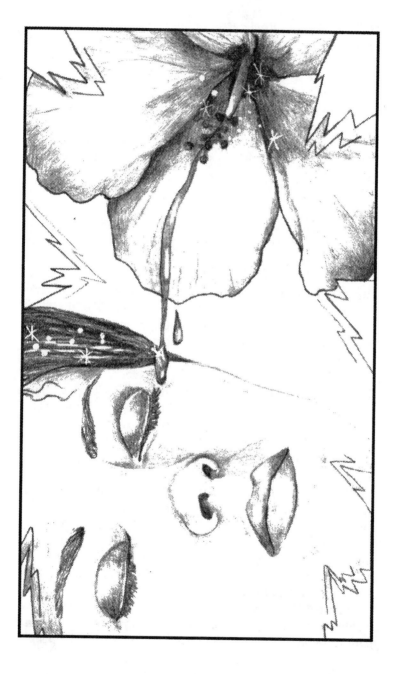

choosing the "wrong" lovers, but now we begin to have mistaken identity. Puck anoints the eye of the youth in "Athenian garments" as directed, but it is the wrong youth. Shakespeare is moving into part two of the three-part structure: the complications of a situation which is opposite that of the "right" one.

Study Questions

1. How did Puck earn his reputation?
2. Why is Oberon angry with Titania?
3. What is her argument with him?
4. What is it Oberon sends Puck to find?
5. How does Oberon intend to punish his wife?
6. Why does Helena pursue Demetrius?
7. Why does Demetrius want Helena to leave him alone?
8. How is it that Oberon is able to overhear them?
9. What does Oberon decide when Puck returns?
10. How does Oberon instruct Puck to recognize Demetrius?

Answers

1. Puck earned his reputation as a hobgoblin by playing pranks, some mean, on both humans and animals as we can see by the fairy's declaring, "…you are that shrewd and knavish sprite…." The name Puck, which is not Robin Goodfellow's actual name, means hobgoblin and often is used interchangeably with the hobgoblin's actual name.

2. Oberon is angry with Titania because she refuses to give up the changeling she has brought with her from India. While she has had many affairs, it is her insistence on keeping the boy that enrages her husband. Oberon, himself, declares, "I do but beg a little changeling boy…" and, more directly, "Give me that boy…."

3. Titania is angry with her husband because she does not want to give up the changeling and she feels Nature "From our

debate, from our dissension..." is turning itself upside down. She maintains that if he would simply allow her to keep the boy the arguing would end and Nature would be able to return to normal.

4. Oberon sends Puck around the world to find a flower called "love-in-idleness" with which to make a love juice. He is going to use this love juice in his plan to punish his wife for keeping the changeling and force her to relinquish the boy to him.

5. Oberon intends to punish his wife by anointing her eye with the love juice while she sleeps so that she will fall in love with the first creature she sees upon waking. He plans to release her from the spell only when she agrees to give him the changeling.

6. Helena pursues Demetrius because she loves him and will "...follow thee and make a heaven of hell to die upon the hand I [Helena] love so well." Demetrius had wooed and won her before Egeus chose him as a son-in-law and before Demetrius fell in love with Hermia. Helena cannot accept that Hermia, who loves and is loved by Lysander, is also loved by Demetrius.

7. Demetrius wants Helena to leave him alone because he is in pursuit of someone himself. He is looking for Hermia and Lysander so that, "The one I'll stay; the other stayeth me," since he thinks he is in love with Hermia and, more importantly, Egeus has chosen him as Hermia's husband.

8. Oberon is invisible, so Helena and Demetrius speak freely in front of him since they do not know he is there. Oberon states that "I am invisible, and I will overhear their conference."

9. When Puck returns, Oberon decides he will help Helena, "a sweet Athenian lady ...in love," by having Puck anoint Demetrius' eye with the love juice just as he, Oberon, will be doing to his wife, Titania. Oberon hopes that Demetrius will fall in love with Helena as she is with Demetrius, whom Oberon calls "a disdainful youth."

10.   Oberon instructs Puck to recognize Demetrius by his "Athenian garments" and gives no further clue as to his identification. This is an excellent example of one of Shakespeare's devices to complicate the plot laid out in Act I.

Suggested Essay Topics

1.   How does Oberon's instructing Puck to anoint the eye of the youth in "Athenian garments" allow Shakespeare to introduce complications to the situation that is opposite of the "right" one?

2.   Considering they are the king and queen of the fairies, explain in your own words why Titania has "... forsworn his [Oberon's] bed and company."

3.   "I love thee not; therefore pursue me not," demands Demetrius of Helena, but she will not desist. How can you explain her actions and Demetrius' reactions in view of Plautus' and Terence's plot structure for love comedies?

Act II, Scene 2

Summary

Titania enters the wood instructing her fairies to sing her to sleep. Just after they do, and leave, Oberon arrives and anoints her eye with the love juice so that she will love the first creature she sees upon waking. Lysander and Hermia make their entrance and decide to sleep since they are so tired that Lysander has forgotten the way to his aunt's house. He lays down next to Hermia but she suggests he move away since they are not yet married. He pretends to be insulted at this request, so she apologizes and rephrases it in such a way that he acquiesces. As they sleep, Puck enters and, thinking he has found the youth in "Athenian garments" who Oberon ordered him to anoint, applies the love juice to Lysander's eye.

Just as Puck leaves, Demetrius arrives with Helena in fast pur-

suit. Helena stops to catch her breath and sees Lysander, who she awakens. He immediately falls in love with her, but she is convinced he is mocking her. Helena believes Lysander is taunting her since she is obviously not the recipient of Demetrius' love as she so desperately wants to be. Lysander rues every minute he's spent with Hermia, upon which Helena—still under the impression that Lysander is making sport of her—leaves in a huff. Lysander sees Hermia and, now loathing her leaves. Hermia awakens from a nightmare calling out his name only to find herself alone and sets out to find him.

Analysis

Here the plot thickens and twists. Oberon has set his plan for revenge on his wife into effect. Puck, thinking he is doing what he was ordered to, manages to alienate the "wrong" choice of husband for Hermia so that he, Lysander, is now in love with Helena. But Helena has been in love with Demetrius all along.

Shakespeare changes the way he uses language when he has spells being cast or characters speaking while spell-bound. The cadence sounds more like song than poetry, and the spells were often sung since they were written in pentameter couplets and other free forms which easily lent themselves to song. In some versions of the play, dances were also introduced during the spell-casting scenes. This scene, in particular, opens with Titania commanding her fairies, "Come, now a roundel and a fairy song ... Sing me now asleep."

The women are passive in this scene, with all of the action being performed by the men: Lysander being anointed and Oberon and Puck doing the anointing. The women passively react in this scene: Titania is anointed because Oberon has chosen to do this to her; Helena is now loved by Lysander and Hermia no longer loved by Lysander because of Puck's annointment. There are no strong women left in the play at this point; even Hippolyta, a queen in her own right, is not an active character because of her love for her captor/fiancé.

These men, who are the aggressors, have managed to thwart their own efforts. Oberon, trying to mend his marriage so that Nature will settle down (according to Titania), plays a terrible trick

on his wife in order to win her love back. Puck, instead of helping Helena win Demetrius, disassociates the true lovers and aligns Lysander with an astonished Helena while Hermia is sure to be heartbroken. Shakespeare is now firmly entrenched in the second part of the three-part structure set up by Plautus and Terence: the complications of the first part.

Study Questions

1. What is it Oberon hopes Titania sees immediately upon wakening?

2. Why does Lysander want to rest?

3. Why does Hermia ask him to move further away to sleep?

4. Why does Robin Goodfellow (Puck) anoint Lysander's eye?

5. What does Robin Goodfellow think Hermia's reason is for sleeping so far removed from Lysander?

6. Why does Helena stop chasing Demetrius?

7. Why does Demetrius leave Helena alone in the wood?

8. Why does Lysander profess his love for Helena?

9. What is Helena's reaction to Lysander's protestations of love?

10. Why does Hermia awake?

Answers

1. Now that Oberon has anointed Titania's eye with the love juice, she will fall in love with the first creature she sees upon waking from the sleep she had instructed the fairies to sing her into. The still angry Oberon hopes Titania will see some "vile thing" the moment she opens her eyes.

2. Lysander wants to rest because Hermia is already "faint with wand'ring in the wood" in the attempt to reach his aunt's house and he, frankly, has forgotten the way and needs to rest himself to remember the way.

3. Hermia, who is running away to avoid her father's choice of husband in order to marry her own—a crime punishable by

death or banishment to a nunnery—asks Lysander, "For my sake, my dear, lie further off yet. Do not lie so near," because it is unseemly for an unmarried couple to sleep together.

4. Puck anoints Lysander's eye because Oberon, being invisible at will, overheard Helena beseech Demetrius to love her and took pity on her. He sent Puck to anoint Demetrius' eye so that he would love Helena since it is obvious she would be the first one he would see upon awakening because she keeps following him. Oberon, however, described Demetrius as the youth in "Athenian garments," which is also what Lysander is wearing. Not knowing this is the wrong person, Puck carries out Oberon's order.

5. Puck thinks Hermia is Helena and that she's sleeping so far from Lysander, who he thinks is Demetrius, because she cannot bring herself to sleep any nearer to "this lack-love, this kill-courtesy."

6. Helena stops chasing Demetrius because he has actually been running away from her and she is "...out of breath in this fond race," and needs to catch her breath.

7. Demetrius leaves Helena alone in the wood "on thy peril," as he thinks, because she will not agree to stop following him and he simply wants to get away from her.

8. Lysander professes his love for Helena because, after Puck anointed his eye with the love juice thinking he was Demetrius, Helena spies him in the wood and wakes him to ascertain if he is "dead or asleep" since she knew he and Hermia had planned to run away the night before. This makes Helena the first creature he saw when he awoke under the spell of the love juice.

9. Helena's reaction to Lysander's pledge of love for her is to demand in anger, "When at your hands did I deserve this scorn?" She thinks he is mocking her since, as far as she knows, he and Hermia are presently in the act of eloping. She feels even worse because it is so obvious that Demetrius loves Hermia, too, even though he had once loved Helena.

10. Hermia awakes because she has a nightmare about a serpent upon her breast. She calls for Lysander to help her, then realizes she is alone, with Lysander being, "Gone? No sound, no word?"

Suggested Essay Topics

1. As Oberon, king of the fairies, carefully present an argument to your wife and queen, Titania, explaining why her past affairs (and yours) did not threaten your marriage but her insistence on keeping this changeling boy rather than conceding to your demands is a threat.

2. Hermia, who is defying Athenian law and facing death or banishment to a nunnery in order to marry the man she loves rather than the man her father chose as her husband, is concerned when Lysander wants to sleep with her in the wood on their way to his aunt's house to be married. She begs him, "Do not lie so near." How may her fears concerning her pristine reputation as a maid (unmarried young woman) be justified at this point in the play?

3. Helena is dumbfounded and hurt when she awakens Lysander in the wood and he professes his love for her, "Yet Hermia still loves you [Lysander]." Carefully, decide why she is dumbfounded and hurt that he would mock her so. Explain this, step by step, to the newly-besotted Lysander. Remember, he is under the spell of the love juice and will not be easily convinced.

Act III

Act III, Scene 1

New Characters:

Peaseblossom, Cobweb, Mote, and Mustardseed: *Titania's fairies*

Summary

The craftsmen meet in the wood to rehearse their play. After finding the perfect setting for the rehearsal, Bottom cautions Quince that he will need two Prologues to the play so that the ladies will not be afraid due to the sword scene or the Lion. The logistics of the moonlight and the need to have someone play the Wall are discussed and the rehearsal begins. This is when Puck (who is invisible), concerned that they are so near the sleeping Titania, makes his entrance to watch and cause mischief. Bottom exits on cue, and while he is "offstage" Puck replaces Bottom's head with that of an ass. When it is Bottom's cue to return, the other craftsmen, seeing his new head, run away in fright. Snout and Quince return separately, but quickly exit again after speaking a few words to Bottom.

Bottom, frightened, sings to keep up his courage. His song wakes up Titania who falls in love with him since her eye had been anointed with the love juice and he is the first creature she sees upon awakening. She calls her fairies to attend to Bottom and he banters with them as each is introduced.

Analysis

Bottom's clownish qualities come forth in full force here. Instead of being frightened by his new situation as Titania's lover, he quickly accepts it as something odd but something he can quickly adjust to and decides Titania is the strange one since she falls in love with him. The humor is in his instantaneous decision to fill the role of her beloved. This is the same man who cautioned that the ladies in the audience will need Prologues to prepare them from the sword scene and the Lion in the play. He now has implicitly reversed his position from one of insisting upon protection for the ladies to that of being the object from which a lady needs to be protected (although he seems unaware he has an ass's head at this time). He soon discovers the lady simply doesn't want protection. He is a stubborn man who refuses to give in to his fear at being alone in a haunted wood and he does not allow his friends to know he is afraid. He thinks they are playing a joke on him and he does not want them to know it has succeeded.

His banter with the fairies is just shy of being rude and makes one wonder if they understand his sly near-insults in the name of humor. He is, however, careful not to be outrightly insulting and, in his peculiar manner, is actually paying tribute to the fairies' powers as spirits. His interchange with Cobweb pulls into play the folklore that cobwebs will staunch the flow of blood when cut. He refers to Peaseblossom's "vegetable" relatives and he teases Mustardseed about the strength of mustard to sting the mouth. His wit is quick, hilariously funny if the point is understood, and clever in view of his present situation. He possesses all the attributes of a contemporary stand-up comic who plays the audience well.

Study Questions

1. Why does Quince feel their rehearsal spot is ideal?

2. Why does Bottom feel they need two Prologues to the play?

3. How do they solve the problems of representing the moonlight and the Wall in their play?

4. Why is Bottom alone when Puck changes his head to that of an ass?

5. How is it that Bottom is alone when Titania awakes?

6. Why hasn't Bottom followed his friends from the wood?

7. Why does Titania awake?

8. What does Titania offer Bottom?

9. What is his reaction to this offer?

10. What part are the fairies to play in this?

Answers

1. Quince feels that the rehearsal spot in the wood is "a marvelous convenient place" for practicing their play because there is a flat area, a green plot, to serve as the stage and shrubs (hawthorne) to represent the tiring house (dressing room).

2. Bottom feels the craftsmen need "a device to make all well" —two Prologues (opening speeches) to the play—to warn the ladies of the audience that there will be a sword scene which is only acting, no one is really going to be hurt, and that the Lion is only an actor, not an actual savage beast who may harm them.

3. The craftsmen solve the problems of the moonlight and the wall by checking the almanac and assuring themselves there will, indeed, be moonlight to shine through the window (casement) on stage the night of the play. "Some man or other must present Wall," is Bottom's suggestion. This actor is to be loam covered and hold his fingers out between Pyramus and Thisbe, who are supposed to be speaking through a wall.

4. Bottom is alone when Puck changes his head to that of an ass because Quince has the actors rehearsing with their stage directions, which are entrances and exits from the stage and the movements they are to make on the stage itself. Bottom has just had an exit cue (word in the script upon which a specified actor performs a predetermined action) and left the green plot serving as the rehearsal stage.

5. Bottom is alone when Titania awakes because during Bottom's exit, Puck—already annoyed that these humans are so close to the sleeping Fairy Queen—decided to play one of his wicked pranks. When Bottom re-enters the green plot with an ass's head instead of his own, his friends run in fright, crying "O monstrous! O strange! We are haunted! Pray, masters, fly, masters! Help!" Although Quince and Snout each return for a moment to attempt to make Bottom understand what has happened, both run away again.

6. Bottom hasn't followed his friends from the wood because he doesn't realize his head has been changed. He thinks their running away and Snout and Quince's attempts to tell him he has changed are nothing more than a joke on him, " ...an attempt to make an ass of me, to fright me if they could." He refuses to run after them and be part of the joke.

7. Titania awakes because Bottom is singing to keep up his courage. He will not admit it to his friends, but he is afraid to be in the wood by himself. He also sings because he wants his friends to hear it, "that they shall hear I am not afraid."

8. Titania offers Bottom the fairies to attend him, jewels, songs sung to lull him into sleep on a bed of pressed flowers, and the chance to, "purge thy mortal grossness so that thou shalt like an airy spirit go."

9. Bottom's reaction to this offer is to banter with the fairies in a clownish way which seems to signify acceptance.

10. The four Fairies—Peaseblossom, Cobweb, Mote, and Mustardseed—are to, "Be kind and courteous to this gentleman [Bottom]," to attend to his every need, to fee him delicacies, and in all ways possible to make him more than comfortable and happy.

Suggested Essay Topics

1. Bottom thinks his friends are playing a trick on him, yet he maintains, "I will walk up and down here, and I will sing, that they shall hear I am not afraid." How is this consistent

with his character as a sensitive, caring, intelligent, buffoon (clown)?

2. Titania implores Bottom, "Out of this wood do not desire to go. Thou shalt remain here whether thou wilt or no." Explain her reasoning in assuming she can order Bottom to feel as she wants him to.

3. As Puck begins his incantation (lines 107–113) to place a spell upon Bottom, what do you specifically notice about the last word in every other line and why do you think Shakespeare changes the way he uses language for spell-casting?

Act III, Scene 2

Summary

Puck reports to Oberon that he placed an ass's head on Bottom and that Titania fell in love with Bottom because he was the first thing she saw when she awoke. Puck also reports that he anointed the eye of the youth in "Athenian garments." When Hermia and Demetrius enter, it becomes obvious to Puck and Oberon that Puck has mistakenly placed the love juice in Lysander's eye, not Demetrius'.

Hermia, finding all other explanations for Lysander's disappearance unacceptable, harasses Demetrius for supposedly murdering Lysander. Demetrius attempts to convince her that he is even more deeply in love with her than he was before and more than Lysander could possibly ever be. Overwhelmed, Demetrius falls asleep when Hermia leaves in disgust. Oberon orders Puck to correct his mistake by finding Helena and then reanointing Demetrius' eye, to make certain she is the one Demetrius falls in love with. As Demetrius sleeps, Oberon annoints his eye with the love juice.

Helena appears pursued by the wooing Lysander. She is convinced he is scorning her with his vows of undying love and is very

angry about this. Their arguing awakens the sleeping Demetrius who also begins to woo the, by now, distraught Helena (the first creature he saw upon awakening after being reanointed with the love juice). Helena is sure the two men have concocted a scheme to make her feel foolish. Hermia joins her friends only to be told by Lysander that he is now in love with Helena, which dumbfounds Hermia. Helena, hearing Hermia deny Lysander's feelings, thinks Hermia is the third party to this elaborate scheme and rails at her longtime friend. Meanwhile, the two men decide the only way to settle who loves Hermia more is to fight a duel. The two men leave to find a spot for their duel. Hermia, beginning to believe Lysander, threatens Helena with bodily harm which causes Helena to run away.

Puck entices Lysander and Demetrius into sleep by tricking them. Puck first pretends to be Demetrius, and then Lysander, in order to tire them out with their efforts to find each other. Helena, tired from running away from Hermia, also appears and falls asleep. Finally, Hermia enters and, tired from trying to find Lysander, falls asleep too. Puck creeps in, reanoints Lysander's eye, and leaves.

Analysis

"Lord, what fools these mortals be!" exclaims Puck in this scene and so it seems since all the complications of the original premise for the play are now in place for the climax: Lysander loves the wrong woman; Puck has anointed the wrong man; Hermia is loved not at all and is in a rage at her childhood friend; and Helena is loved by both men—one who she doesn't want and the other she does love but cannot believe he loves her—and she is fearful of the hatred of her childhood friend, Hermia.

Innocent mistaken identity, in this case Puck's mistaking Lysander for Demetrius since both were wearing "Athenian garments," is common in Shakespeare's plays. What adds even more to Shakespeare's humor in this scene is the fairies seeing the humans as interchangeable, whereas each humans feel themselves unique. While the situations may seem somewhat contrived to a modern audience, those watching the play when it was first performed surely accepted the error easily and enjoyed the unfolding of the plot.

The range of emotions in just one scene is quite wide. Poor Hermia goes from being the beloved of Lysander to the woman scorned in, literally, the blink of an eye. In addition, Hermia fears for Lysander's life and feels hate for her best friend, Helena. In the same scene, Helena loses her best friend, the lover she pursues, and gained a lover she never wanted. Helena completely misconstrues the love of the two men as an elaborate joke meant to hurt her and is baffled as to how her friends could do this to her. Demetrius and Lysander seem not to question the changes in their feelings and are not as perplexed as the women. In addition, if you read carefully, you will see that in their arguments, Shakespeare manages to have the four young people sling racial insults at each other; while this was perfectly acceptable and expected in his time, today it is considered politically incorrect.

Study Questions

1. What is it Puck reports to Oberon?

2. Why is Hermia following Demetrius?

3. What is it Oberon realizes when he sees them together?

4. How is this mistake to be rectified?

5. Why won't Helena accept Lysander's advances?

6. Why does she doubt the veracity of Demetrius' protestations of love?

7. Why do Hermia and Helena argue?

8. Why do each of the young people leave?

9. How does Puck manage to make Lysander and Demetrius sleep?

10. Why do Helena and Hermia also fall asleep?

Answers

1. Puck reports to Oberon that he came upon the craftsmen "met together to rehearse a play" near the sleeping Titania and changed Bottom's head for that of an ass, then made certain Bottom was near Titania so that he was the first be-

ing she saw when she woke up and would she fall in love with him. Puck also mentions how frightened Bottom's friends were and that the eye of the youth in "Athenian garments" has also been anointed.

2. Hermia is following Demetrius because she is convinced Demetrius, "...hath slain Lysander in his sleep..." Both men want to marry her. Theseus has ordered her to marry Demetrius, as Egeus desires, or face the nunnery or death. She and Lysander have run away to elope. She cannot think of another reason for Lysander to leave her sleeping, alone and unguarded, in the haunted wood other than that Demetrius must have killed Lysander.

3. When Oberon sees Hermia and Demetrius together, he realizes that while Demetrius is the youth he'd wanted Puck to anoint with the love juice, Hermia is not the maid he'd seen pursuing Demetrius; the maid he wanted to help by having the man she was pursuing fall in love with her. In his dismay, he cries to Puck, "What hast thou done?"

4. The mistake is to be rectified by having Puck, "about the wood go swifter than the wind, and Helena of Athens look thou find," bringing her to Oberon, in the haunted wood. Once Helena is found Oberon and Puck will make Demetrius fall asleep and reanoint his eye so that he would fall in love with Helena, instead of Hermia.

5. Helena will not accept Lysander's advances because—as she says—"These vows are Hermia's." In addition, Lysander and Hermia just told her the previous night that they were eloping. Helena is in love with Demetrius, no one else. Hermia is both her best and childhood friend, and this seems like a case of mocking to her. She is hurt, bewildered, and angry about his advances.

6. Helena doubts the veracity of Demetrius' love because he had loved her once before and left. He has been in love with Hermia, as far as she knows, since he came to Athens so that Egeus could have Theseus force Hermia to marry him rather than face a nunnery or death. Helena suspects he is part of

this cruel joke to mock her love of him. She is baffled at the two men's behavior and wonders at them "...but you must join in souls to mock me too?"

7. Hermia and Helena argue because Helena is convinced Hermia, her closest and oldest friend, is "...one of this confederacy..." to mock her. They are also arguing because Hermia is convinced Helena is scorning her by refusing Lysander's love after somehow managing to make him fall in love with her (Helena) and, hence, out of love with herself (Hermia).

8. Each of the young people leaves for a different reason. Helena, physically afraid of the smaller Hermia, comments to Hermia, "My legs are longer though, to run away," and does so. Hermia, incensed and devastated, pursues Helena. Demetrius and Lysander, losing all hope of convincing Helena which one of them loves her more, go off to find a location for the duel which will supposedly prove to Helena which one loves her more.

9. Puck manages to trick Demetrius and Lysander and make them sleep by tiring them each out. He tricks each of them by pretending to be the other and throwing his voice, as each of them, hither, and yon. They keep running from here to there to find the other and are finally exhausted into sleep as Demetrius explains in saying, "Faintness constraineth me to measure out my length on this cold bed..."

10. Hermia and Helena fall asleep because they, too, are exhausted. Hermia has been trying to catch Helena as Helena runs away from her. This after a night of nightmares for Hermia and running after Demetrius for Helena. Helena concisely states the situation when she murmurs, "Never so weary, never so in woe...," before falling asleep.

Suggested Essay Topics

1. As a contemporary of Helena, how would you make each of your friends understand your feelings about what you consider their conspiracy "...to conjure tears up in a poor maid's

eyes with your [their] derision!" Remember to keep the situation the same as it is in the play, even though you are modernizing Helena's communication methods.

2. As Hermia, you have just lost your love to your best friend who you think has "stol'n my love's heart from him. . .." This would mean losing your best friend too. Which is the worse tragedy and why? Use not only your own feelings but validations from the play to prove your point.

3. How is it possible that neither Lysander nor Demetrius took their loves' feelings into account when each of these men decided who they would love, as demonstrated by Lysander's confusion when asking, "Why should you think that I should woo in scorn?" You will need to carefully peruse the play for proof to support your opinion.

Act IV

Act IV, Scene 1

Summary

Bottom makes several absurd requests of the fairies as he and Titania chatter about whether to eat or sleep. They choose to sleep. Oberon and Puck come upon them while they sleep as Oberon explains to Puck that he is now in possession of the changeling and will take the spell from Titania. He does so, wakes her, and she is instantly in love with her husband, Oberon, again and repulsed by the ass-headed Bottom whom she had so recently adored. Oberon orders Puck to take the ass's head from Bottom and Puck complies as Titania causes Bottom, Helena, Hermia, Demetrius, and Lysander to fall far more deeply asleep than they already are.

Theseus, Hippolyta, and Egeus arrive accompanied by the sound of hunting horns which awakens the five sleepers, but not before the three new arrivals notice the sleepers and wonder why they are there. After Theseus has them awakened, he questions them to no avail. Lysander remembers he and Hermia were going to elope, but nothing more. Egeus is outraged to hear this and insists Theseus punish both Lysander and Hermia for disobeying his order that she marry Demetrius who now announces he no longer

wants to marry Hermia since he realizes it is Helena he loves. Theseus, seeing a solution to the problem of having to punish Hermia, overrides Egeus and announces that the two couples will be married during his own marriage to Hippolyta.

The two young couples are not certain if they dreamt what happened or if this was reality. As they compare their experiences, they agree the reality is that the duke, Hippolyta, and Egeus were there and ordered Hermia and Lysander, and Helena and Demetrius to join them at the temple. They intend to continue comparing their dreams on the way. Bottom awakes abruptly, thinking he is awaiting his cue during the rehearsal. He acknowledges that he is alone, and resolves to have Quince turn his "dream" into a ballad to sing at the end of the play the craftsmen will be presenting at the revel.

Analysis

As dictated by Plautus and Terence, Shakespeare reverses the opening situation and cleverly reunites each couple: Helena is once again beloved by Demetrius who she has never stopped pursuing; Hermia has her Lysander returned to her; Titania loves her Oberon again; and Theseus and Hippolyta will be married just as they planned except that they will have the other two couples marrying at their own wedding. Those who are not couples also have resolution of one kind or another: Bottom is delighted that he will have a dream for Quince to make a ballad about; Theseus finds a solution to his problem of either having to kill or banish his friend's daughter; and Puck, having corrected his mistakes, is no longer in Oberon's bad graces.

It is apparent there is one dissatisfied, unresolved character in the play: Egeus. His daughter will neither marry the man he has chosen, Demetrius (because Hermia loves Lysander, and Demetrius is now in love with Helena), nor will she be punished by either banishment to a nunnery or death for breaking the Athenian law stating she must marry her father's choice of husband. The duke, to whom he has brought Lysander, Demetrius, and Hermia for "justice," has declared that the two young couples share his own wedding.

Study Questions

1. What is it Bottom asks Peaseblossom, Mustardseed, and Cobweb to do?

2. What news does Oberon tell Puck?

3. Why is Titania in love with her husband again?

4. Why are Theseus, Hippolyta, and Egeus in the wood?

5. Why does Theseus think the five sleeping people came to the wood?

6. What does Lysander answer when questioned by Theseus?

7. Why is Egeus so angry?

8. Why won't Demetrius marry Hermia as he had promised?

9. What is Theseus' decision?

10. Why does Bottom want Quince to write a ballad?

Answers

1. Bottom asks Peaseblossom to scratch his head. He asks Cobweb to bring him the unbroken honey-bag of a red-hipped bumble-bee on top of a thistle (a type of flower). He then asks Mustardseed to help Cobweb scratch since Bottom, still unaware he has an ass' head, ironically mentions, "And I am such a tender ass, if my hair do but tickle me, I must scratch," while thinking it's time to get to a barber's for a shave.

2. Oberon tells Puck the news that Titania, Oberon's wife and queen of the fairies, has given him the changeling once she fell in love with Bottom (due to the love juice). Now that he has the changeling she had previously refused to relinquish, he orders Puck to remove the spell from Titania's eye and, "...take this transformed scalp from off the head of this Athenian swain..."

3. Titania is in love with her husband, Oberon—king of the fairies —again because the spell was removed from her once she gave Oberon the changeling from India. "O! How my eyes do loathe his visage now!" she says of Bottom and has a dif-

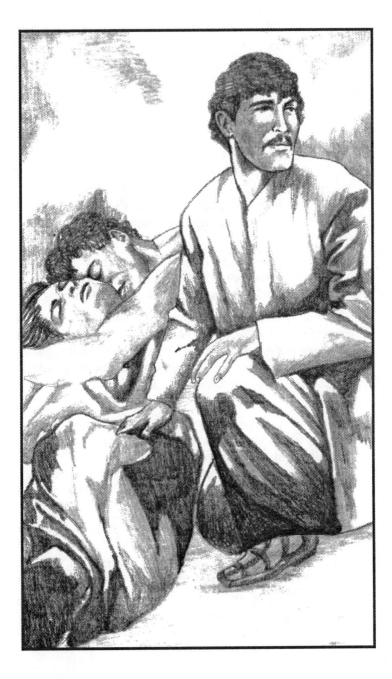

ficult time understanding she had been in love with him while under the love-juice spell.

4. Theseus, Hippolyta, and Egeus have come to the wood to hunt as a way of starting the May Day celebration. Theseus also wants Hippolyta to hear "the music of my hounds," since this was considered a sort of music at the time.

5. Theseus thinks the five sleeping people— Bottom, Lysander, Hermia, Helena, and Demetrius—came to the wood to begin the rites to celebrate May Day. He also reminds Egeus that this is the day Hermia is to "...give answer of her choice": to marry the man her father chose as her husband, be banished to a nunnery, or be put to death.

6. When questioned by Theseus, Lysander answers that he really doesn't know how he came to be in the wood, but he does remember that he and Hermia's "intent was to be gone from Athens ...without the peril of the Athenian law –."

7. Egeus is so angry because Lysander has just admitted he and Hermia are defying the Athenian law which demands that a daughter marry the man her father chooses for her. Elopement with another man is not one of the daughter's options; therefore, Egeus now declares, "...I beg the law, the law, upon his head."

8. Demetrius will not marry Hermia as he promised because, "the object and the pleasure of mine eye, is only Helena," due to Oberon and the love juice's intervention. Oberon told Puck to make certain Helena was the first creature Demetrius saw when he awakened after Puck reanointed his eye with the love juice while Demetrius was sleeping.

9. Theseus' decision is that the two couples in love—Lysander and Hermia, and Demetrius and Helena—"...shall eternally be knit –," during his own wedding to Hippolyta. Egeus is not pleased with this decision but, since he came to his duke asking for a judgment, he cannot argue.

10. Bottom wants Quince to write a ballad about his dream, as he clearly states when he simply says, "I will get Peter Quince

to write a ballad of this dream." What he now thinks was a dream was really his experience while he had an ass's head. Bottom would like to hear the ballad of this dream/experience presented at the end of the play the craftsmen are performing the night of the wedding ceremonies.

Suggested Essay Topics

1. As Egeus, what are your particular thoughts on being robbed of what you perceive as justice from the duke to whom you have said, "...My lord, you have enough. I beg the law, the law, upon his head." Be certain to include the Athenian law about a father choosing his daughter's husband, your friendship with Duke Theseus, your great dislike for the cheating Lysander, your bewilderment with Demetrius' change of heart, and your utter frustration at your daughter's refusal to obey.

2. Duke Theseus seems relieved at not having to punish Hermia, as he decrees to Egeus, "...I will overbear your will..." Considering he is the highest authority, how can you explain these unexpected feelings. Keep in mind that he, himself, is being married to Hippolyta that night.

3. Bottom makes many references to his ass-like behavior without ever acknowledging that his head is now that of an ass. What are these references and how may they be interpreted as describing either the animal's behavior or that of a person acting as an ass—that is, poorly or stupidly? Use the text as your resource material.

Act IV, Scene 2

Summary

The craftsmen regret the loss of Bottom, for only he could play the role of Pyramus. Without him, they cannot perform the play.

Snug arrives to tell them that two other couples are also being married that night and, were they performing, they would have made their fortunes. Bottom arrives, refusing to tell them what has happened until later, but offering them advice on their roles for their play which has been chosen for the night's revel.

Analysis

It appears that while Bottom is clownish and egotistical, his friends truly like him and rue his disappearance—not only for his acting, but for who he is. Bottom is in all probability a lover, too, since Quince—an intelligent man and Bottom's friend—inadvertently uses "paramour" or lover in his accolades to Bottom instead of the correct word, paragon, and is unaware of his error until corrected by Flute. Bottom, in turn, appears to truly care for his friends as is demonstrated by his deferring his own tale until after the play so that they may spend the rest of the day preparing (following his advice to the actors, of course, even though Quince is the director) and his obvious happiness that it is their play is chosen for the revel.

Study Questions

1. How do the actors know Bottom has not yet returned?
2. Why can't they perform the play?
3. What do his friends say are Bottom's best qualities?
4. What mistake does Quince make in referring to Bottom's voice?
5. What is Snug's news?
6. What is especially disappointing about not being able to present the play?
7. What would Flute have demanded for Bottom?
8. What is Bottom's reaction upon finding his friends?
9. Why won't he tell them what has happened to him?
10. What is his advice to his fellow actors?

Answers

1. The actors know Bottom has not yet returned because Robin Starveling went to his house, only to find, "He [Bottom] cannot be heard of."

2. They can't perform the play because there is not, "...a man in all Athens able to discharge Pyramus but he [Bottom]."

3. His friends say Bottom's best qualities are his wit (sense of humor), which is "the best wit of any handicraftsman in Athens," and his sweet voice.

4. The mistake Quince makes is in referring to Bottom's voice as that of a "paramour" rather than "paragon." The humor in this is that a paramour is a lover, while a paragon is a model of excellence. The bawdy joke is that Quince is calling his friend a lover, rather than a role model.

5. Snug's news is that, "...there is two or three lords and ladies more married," that night.

6. What is especially disappointing about not being able to perform that night is that with the additional couples being married, the craftsmen, "...had all been made men," from just this one night's performance. This means they would have made enough money to live comfortable lives.

7. Flute declares he would have demanded nothing less than six pence – quite a bit of money at that time – for Bottom's performance or he'd "be hanged."

8. Bottom's reaction upon finding his friends is to ask the group in general why they are so sad.

9. Bottom will not tell his friends what has happened to him because, since it is so fantastic, it will take a long time to tell and they need the time to prepare for their performance that night because their play has been chosen for the revel. Bottom saves his tale, for he would prefer, "no more words."

10. Bottom's advice to his fellow actors is as follows: prepare your costumes; review your parts; Thisbe—wear clean clothes; Lion—do not cut your fingernails so that they may some-

what resemble claws; and, "eat no onions nor garlic," before the performance.

Suggested Essay Topics

1. Bottom is actually making a jest when he directs his fellow actors to refrain from eating onions or garlic before the performance so that the audience will say their play, "is a sweet comedy." In reality, how is the play-within-the-play "a sweet comedy"? Use documentation from within the text.

2. Upon waking, Bottom explains to himself, "I have had a dream past the wit of man to say what dream it was." How is this Shakespeare's way of having a human interpret the fairy world? Look for validations to correctly explain Bottom's quote.

3. Demetrius queries, "Are you sure that we are awake? It seems to me that yet we sleep, we dream." How is this an alternate explanation for a human's visit to the fairy world of spells and being enchanted? Remember to include what would be absurd behavior on Demetrius' part were he not under a fairy spell.

Act V

Act V, Scene 1

Summary

Hippolyta and Theseus think the lovers are telling them a fantasy rather than what really happened to them in the haunted wood. The lovers join them and Theseus asks Philostrate what entertainment is available to them during the three hours between their wedding feast and bedtime. Theseus rejects one suggestion after another, deciding upon the craftsmen's play. Philostrate tries to dissuade him from this choice by telling him it is inane, but Philostrate does have to admit he laughed until he cried when he saw how terrible it was.

The craftsmen present their play much to the delight of their audience, who freely pass comments from one to another and discourse with the actors in the midst of their play. The actors are complimented on their skills and asked questions as they act and the audience critiques and discusses the actors' roles and intents throughout the play. At the finish of the play, Bottom asks Theseus if he would prefer the Epilogue or a dance. Theseus chooses the dance. The dance is performed, the players (actors) exit, and Theseus announces it is time for all to retire.

Oberon, Titania, and the fairies take over the night intending to sing and dance until daybreak. But first, Oberon sends the fair-

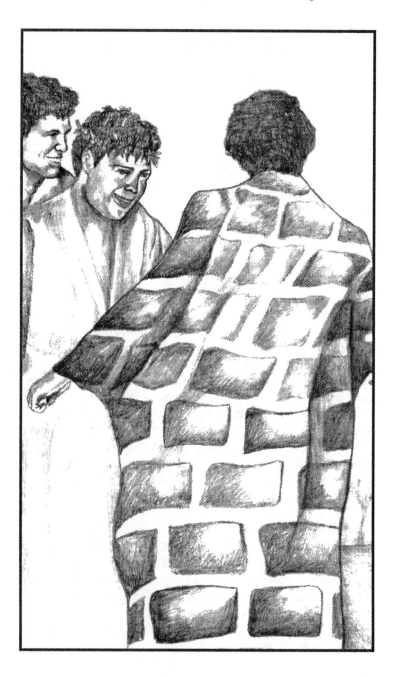

ies to bless each of the newly married couples and whatever children they might have. Puck remains behind to beg the audience's forgiveness for any offense given and for their applause.

Analysis

Shakespeare has neatly tied up all his loose ends by having the craftsmen present their play-within-the-play. The craftsmen's play is a dramatist's and actor's worst nightmare: unexpected laughter, disparaging remarks, cues missed, lines forgotten, overacting, and loud comments by the audience. It also makes the point that the lovers—Demetrius and Helena (who were what we now call "off again, on again"), Hermia and Lysander (whose union was opposed by Hermia's father), Theseus and Hippolyta (who met while leading opposing armies), and Oberon and Titania (who both had extramarital affairs)—have each other in the end, unlike the unfortunate Pyramus and Thisbe. In addition, it makes clear that the players, much as Shakespeare's own company, owed allegiance to their patrons and were thankful for the patronage.

Study Questions

1. Why does Theseus doubt the reality of the story the lovers tell him?

2. What are the choices for the revel?

3. Why does Theseus choose the craftsmen's play?

4. What is the consensus of opinion about the Prologue?

5. Why does Theseus command Demetrius to be silent?

6. What is Hippolyta's astute comment about the play?

7. How does Robin Starveling defend the use of the lanthorn (lantern) in representing the moon?

8. How does Pyramus die in the play-within-the-play?

9. What does Oberon tell the fairies to do before they sing and dance all night?

10. What two things does Puck ask from the audience before Shakespeare's play ends?

Answers

1. Theseus calls the story the lovers tell him, "More strange than true," because he thinks, "the lunatic, the lover, and the poet," are alike in their overblown imaginations. Hippolyta wonders if this is true since all of the four lovers tell the same story.

2. The choices for the revel are a battle song sung by, "an Athenian eunuch [a castrated male] to the harp," an old play Theseus has already seen, another play he deems too serious for a wedding feast, and the craftsmen's play.

3. Theseus chooses the craftsmen's play for several reasons. The first is he doesn't care for the other choices for various reasons. The second is he is intrigued by the contradictory wording of the title: "A tedious brief scene of young Pyramus and his love Thisbe, very tragical mirth." He is also delighted that his craftsmen would honor him by attempting to push their brains to write a play and then their acting skills by presenting it.

4. The consensus of opinion about the Prologue is that it was roughly and poorly delivered, but Lysander takes this as a morality lesson that, "it is not enough to speak, but to speak true," if one is to bother speaking at all.

5. Theseus commands Demetrius to be silent because. "Pyramus draws near the wall," and he, Theseus, wants to hear if he and Thisbe do speak through the Wall (portrayed by Snout).

6. Hippolyta's astute comment about the play is, "This is the silliest stuff that ever I heard."

7. Starveling defends the use of the lanthorn in representing the moon by saying, "The lanthorn doth the horned moon present," three times and offering no other explanation.

8. Pyramus dies in the play-within-the-play when he kills himself, proclaiming, "Out, sword, and wound the pap of Pyramus. . .." He had found Thisbe's bloodied mantle (cloak) and concluded the Lion killed her, which is not the case at

all. Since, according to Pyramus' thinking, she is dead and he is her love, he sees no reason to continue living.

9. Oberon tells the fairies that before they sing and dance all night, they are to bless the newly married couples and whatever children these couples may have in the future so that they, the humans, "...ever shall be fortunate."

10. The two things Puck asks of the audience before Shakespeare's play ends are that they forgive the characters for any offense given and that they applaud or, "Give me your hands...."

Suggested Essay Topics

1. Theseus likens, "the lunatic, the lover, and the poet," in his explanation to Hippolyta of why he thinks the lovers are recounting a fantasy rather than what really happened to them in the haunted wood. Today, we often make the same comparison in our own ways. Examine your life, or that of someone you know, to prove either the truth or falsehood of this statement. Remember to keep referring to facts from the text to support your argument.

2. As a modern audience member, how would you react to the comments of the audience in the play-within-the-play and their interaction with the actors as they were on stage? Use the text for specific examples to illustrate your opinion.

3. In the play-within-the-play, Pyramus commits suicide when he thinks his love is dead. This is a common theme in plays (to wit, Shakespeare's own *Romeo and Juliet*). How is it possible that the one committing suicide does not verify the death of his/her lover before killing him/herself? Use the lovers in *A Midsummer Night's Dream* as examples to illustrate your thoughts on this topic.

Sample Analytical Paper Topics

Topic #1

It is only in the last few decades that the position of women in society has been reexamined. From reading Shakespeare's plays, we have some information about their negative treatment in the 1500s and 1600s. What, precisely, was this negative treatment of women to which we no longer adhere?

Outline

I. Thesis Statement: *In* A Midsummer Night's Dream, *William Shakespeare demonstrates the negative treatment women received from society in the sixteenth and seventeenth centuries.*

II. Owned by Father

    A. Father has the right to choose daughter's husband

    B. Failure of daughter to comply with father's choice will lead to either death or banishment to a nunnery

III. Unable to Choose Husband

    A. See II.

    B. Hermia faces death or banishment be eloping with Lysander

    C. Hippolyta won in battle by Theseus

IV.   Friendships Dependent upon Mate

    A.   Hermia hates Helena because Lysander loves Helena

    B.   Helena wants to be like Hermia because Demetrius loves Hermia

V.   Hypocrisy in Sexual Values

    A.   Hermia asks Lysander not to sleep so close to her in the wood since they are not yet married although they are in the act of eloping

    B.   Although married, Oberon and Titania freely have affairs

Topic #2

People are commonly referred to as "ass" when they behave poorly or stupidly. How has William Shakespeare exemplified such behavior by having Robin Goodfellow (Puck) replace Nick Bottom's head with that of the animal, an ass?

Outline:

I.   Thesis Statement: *In* A Midsummer Night's Dream, *William Shakespeare demonstrates the appropriateness of certain animal labels to describe human behavior—to wit, Bottom's having an ass's head.*

II.   The Qualities of Bottom's Character Which are Similar to Those of the Animal, An Ass

    A.   Stubbornness as he refuses to allow his friends to see his fear at being alone in the haunted wood

    B.   Casual awareness of his sexuality when Titania courts him

    C.   Coarse hair of which he complains to the fairies without realizing he possesses an ass's head

III.   Bottom's Denial of his Feelings

    A.   Refuses to join his friends when they flee the haunted wood for fear they will know he realizes (or thinks he realizes) they are making a jest of him

    B.   Whistles for courage rather than admit his fear when he finds himself in the haunted wood alone

  C. Thinks his experience was a dream while probably feeling it was real

IV. Lack of Examination of New Situations

  A. Blindly accepts the role of Titania's lover

  B. After being freed of Puck's spell, doesn't question why his body no longer has the lightness of a fairy's

V. Mocks Others

  A. Refers to a cobweb's ability to staunch the flow of blood from a cut when introduced to Cobweb

  B. Asks Peaseblossom to remember him to his vegetable family members when introduced to him

  C. Refers to mustard's ability to burn the mouth when introduced to Mustardseed

  D. Uses this mockery to pay tribute to the fairies' attributes

VI. Takes Advantage of Others

  A. Tells Mustardseed and Peaseblossom to scratch his face

  B. Sends Cobweb on a quest to find a particular kind of bee with a particular kind of honey on a particular flower and to bring the honey-bag back to him unbroken

Topic #3

 In life, people will often experience trials and tribulations before they eventually arrive at their destination—be it with their career, relationship, or family. While Egeus and Hermia do not appear reconciled at the end of the play, each of the lovers are united or reunited with their true loves.

Outline

I. Thesis Statement: *The characters in William Shakespeare's A Midsummer Night's Dream are successful, after many trials and tribulations, in acquiring their desired relationships.*

II. Hermia and Lysander

    A.   Must go to Athens with Egeus for Duke Theseus' decision

    B.   Demetrius competes with Lysander for Hermia's hand in marriage and has Egeus' approval

    C.   Hermia and Lysander decide to defy the law and elope

    D.   Their elopement is aborted

    E.   Lysander is temporarily charmed into loving Helena

    F.   Hermia accuses Helena of "stealing" Lysander's love

III. Helena and Demetrius

    A.   Demetrius at one time loved Helena, but later left her

    B.   Demetrius is in love with Hermia and has her father's approval

    C.   Helena is temporarily loved by Lysander when he is under the spell of the love juice

    D.   Hermia accuses Helena of "stealing" Lysander's love

IV. Hippolyta and Theseus

    A.   Theseus is the Duke of Athens

    B.   Hippolyta is the Queen of the Amazons

    C.   Theseus captured her in battle

V. Titania and Oberon

    A.   Each has extra-marital affairs

    B.   Titania refuses to relinquish the changeling she's brought with her from India

    C.   Oberon places a spell on his wife

    D.   Titania falls in love with an ass-headed human, Bottom

Topic #4

    Friendship has a way of lasting despite misunderstandings, arguments, different opinions, and time. William Shakespeare demonstrates this via the ebb and flow of the four lovers' relationships in *A Midsummer Night's Dream*.

Outline

I. Thesis Statement: *In* A Midsummer Night's Dream, *William Shakespeare demonstrates the enduring quality of friendship*

II. Helena and Hermia

   A. Harmony as childhood friends and when Hermia tells Helena of her elopement so that Helena will be reassured that Hermia will no longer be available for Demetrius to marry

   B. Conflict in that Demetrius first loves Helena, then Hermia, then Helena again and also when Lysander is charmed into loving Helena

   C. Reconciliation when each is united with her proper love

III. Lysander and Demetrius

   A. No initial contact nor feeling about each other

   B. Conflict in that both want to marry Hermia but Demetrius has Egeus' approval to marry Hermia while Lysander has her love. Lysander plans to elope with Hermia. Both men jilt Hermia, loving Helena, while under the love-juice's spell, which prompts them to plan a duel to win Helena's hand

   C. Reconciliation when reunited with their chosen lovers

IV. Demetrius and Hermia

   A. Harmony when Demetrius had previously been wooing Hermia's childhood friend, Helena

   B. Conflict in that Demetrius plans to marry Hermia (with her father's approval) while she plans to elope with Lysander. Also conflict that he jilted Helena to woo Hermia

   C. Reconciliation, with the love juice's help, when Demetrius falls in love with Helena again

V. Lysander and Helena

    A. Harmony when Lysander plans to elope with Helena's closest friend, Hermia, which would no longer allow Demetrius to marry Hermia

    B. Conflict when Lysander temporarily falls in love with Helena while under the love juice's spell and, again, when Lysander calls Helena nasty names during her argument with Hermia

    C. Reconciliation when Lysander is reunited with Hermia and Helena with Demetrius

SECTION EIGHT

Bibliography

Bloom, Harold, ed. Modern Critical Interpretations: *William Shakespeare's A Midsummer Night's Dream*. New York: Chelsea House Publishing, 1987.

Charney, Maurice. *All of Shakespeare*. New York: Columbia University Press, 1993.

Foakes, R. A. ed. *The New Cambridge Shakespeare*. New York: Cambridge University Press, 1984.

Goddard, Harold C. *The Meaning of Shakespeare—Volume 1*. Illinois: University of Chicago Press, 1951.

Gurr, Andrew. *Playgoing in Shakespeare's London*. New York: Cambridge University Press, 1987.

Halliday, F.E. *Shakespeare*. New York: Thames and Hudson, Inc., 1956.

Levi, Peter. *The Life and Times of William Shakespeare*. New York: Henry Holt and Company, 1988.

Macdonald, Ronald R. *Twayne's English Author Series—William Shakespeare: The Comedies*. New York: Macmillan Publishing Company, 1992.

Mowat, Barbara A. & Paul Werstine, ed. *The New Folger Library—Shakespeare: A Midsummer Night's Dream*. New York: Washington Square Press, 1993.

Schoenbaum, S. William *Shakespeare: A Compact Documentary Life*. New York: Oxford University Press, Inc., 1977.

Schoenbaum, S. *Shakespeare's Lives*. New York: Oxford University Press, 1991.

REA's Test Preps
The Best in Test Preparation

- REA "Test Preps" are **far more** comprehensive than any other test preparation series
- Each book contains up to **eight** full-length practice tests based on the most recent exams
- **Every** type of question likely to be given on the exams is included
- Answers are accompanied by **full** and **detailed** explanations

REA publishes over 60 Test Preparation volumes in several series. They include:

Advanced Placement Exams(APs)
Biology
Calculus AB & Calculus BC
Chemistry
Computer Science
Economics
English Language & Composition
English Literature & Composition
European History
Government & Politics
Physics B & C
Psychology
Spanish Language
Statistics
United States History

College-Level Examination Program (CLEP)
Analyzing and Interpreting Literature
College Algebra
Freshman College Composition
General Examinations
General Examinations Review
History of the United States I
History of the United States II
Human Growth and Development
Introductory Sociology
Principles of Marketing
Spanish

SAT II: Subject Tests
Biology E/M
Chemistry
English Language Proficiency Test
French
German

SAT II: Subject Tests (cont'd)
Literature
Mathematics Level IC, IIC
Physics
Spanish
United States History
Writing

Graduate Record Exams (GREs)
Biology
Chemistry
Computer Science
General
Literature in English
Mathematics
Physics
Psychology

ACT - ACT Assessment

ASVAB - Armed Services Vocational Aptitude Battery

CBEST - California Basic Educational Skills Test

CDL - Commercial Driver License Exam

CLAST - College Level Academic Skills Test

COOP & HSPT - Catholic High School Admission Tests

ELM - California State University Entry Level Mathematics Exam

FE (EIT) - Fundamentals of Engineering Exams - For both AM & PM Exams

FTCE - Florida Teacher Certification Exam

GED - High School Equivalency Diploma Exam (U.S. & Canadian editions)

GMAT CAT - Graduate Management Admission Test

LSAT - Law School Admission Test

MAT - Miller Analogies Test

MCAT - Medical College Admission Test

MTEL - Massachusetts Tests for Educator Licensure

MSAT - Multiple Subjects Assessment for Teachers

NJ HSPA - New Jersey High School Proficiency Assessment

NYSTCE: LAST & ATS-W - New York State Teacher Certification

PLT - Principles of Learning & Teaching Tests

PPST - Pre-Professional Skills Tests

PSAT - Preliminary Scholastic Assessment Test

SAT I - Reasoning Test

TExES - Texas Examinations of Educator Standards

THEA - Texas Higher Education Assessment

TOEFL - Test of English as a Foreign Language

TOEIC - Test of English for International Communication

USMLE Steps 1,2,3 - U.S. Medical Licensing Exams

U.S. Postal Exams 460 & 470

RESEARCH & EDUCATION ASSOCIATION
61 Ethel Road W. • Piscataway, New Jersey 08854
Phone: (732) 819-8880   **website: www.rea.com**

Please send me more information about your Test Prep books

Name _____

Address _____

City _____ State _____ Zip _____